ICHIMOKU TR

How To Profit From Its Unfair Advantages

JARROD SANDERS

I0065426

Copyright © 2022 Jarrod Sanders - All rights reserved.

Legal Notice

This book or parts thereof may not be reproduced in any form, stored in any retrieval system, or transmitted in any form by any means—electronic, mechanical, photocopy, recording, or otherwise—without prior written permission of the publisher, except as provided by United States of America copyright law and fair use.

Disclaimer Notice

The publisher and the author do not make any guarantee or other promise as to any results that may be obtained from using the content of this book. You should never make any investment decision without first consulting with your own financial advisor and conducting your own research and due diligence. To the maximum extent permitted by law, the publisher and the author disclaim any and all liability in the event any information, commentary, analysis, opinions, advice and/or recommendations contained in this book prove to be inaccurate, incomplete or unreliable, or result in any investment or other losses.

Although the publisher and the author have made every effort to ensure that the information in this book was correct at press time and while this publication is designed to provide accurate information in regard to the subject matter covered, the publisher and the author assume no responsibility for errors, inaccuracies, omissions, or any other inconsistencies herein and hereby disclaim any liability to any party for any loss, damage, or disruption caused by errors or omissions, whether such errors or omissions result from negligence, accident, or any other cause.

TABLE OF CONTENTS

INTRODUCTION

Have you faced with loss after loss and become tired of finding a good trading system?

If the answer is Yes, you're not alone. Chances are that many traders are struggling with their trade system, and a reliable trading strategy might be one of the most annoying headaches to traders.

The truth is that there are too many tools available in the financial market. This might seem positive at first glance, but it also confuses you in finding one that truly works. We've been told a lot about price action, stochastics, moving average, support & resistance, and much more. However, most of the tools out there reflect the market in just a few aspects without giving us a comprehensive understanding of identifying trade opportunities, entries, and exit points. One of the scare exceptions (if not the only one) is Ichimoku Kinko Hyo which I want to call *a complete trading system*.

Ichimoku Kinko Hyo originated in Japan in the 1930s and has been spreading all over the world for the past decades. It has been recognized for its effectiveness in determining high-probability price targets based on past price behaviors. Being an indispensable tool to many traders, especially Japanese ones, Ichimoku has its own voice in identifying the market structure and analyzing price action from short-term to long-term view.

I've been trading with Ichimoku since the early days of my trading career (nearly two decades ago), and I must say Ichimoku is unique in its own way, with lots of time periods taken into account to give a comprehensive view of the market while eliminating risk areas. It takes time to get to where I am today in terms of using Ichimoku effectively while saving time. However, one thing I can assure you: you can save tons of time and shorten your way to success with the help of what I convey in this book. This is the biggest motivation for me to write this book – the one I'm extremely proud of.

I tend not to call Ichimoku Kinko Hyo an indicator, but a *toolset*. This toolset includes two parts: (1) the five lines and (2) theories. The former is more popular among traders because it is incorporated into the visual Ichimoku system. However, failing to explore and apply the three theories (time theory, wave theory, and price theory) would be a big mistake for anyone wanting to make the best of Ichimoku Kinko Hyo.

We'll go step-by-step through each component within the toolset via a lot of illustrations and chart examples so that you can fully grasp the idea of the investor. Also, we've tried to connect as many aspects as possible so that you can gain a comprehensive view of the market. Nearly 100 chart examples are included so that you can be in the best position to understand what I present. The strategies are what I accumulated and optimized for the last 15 years. You can definitely make some adjustments to suit your style. Yet, even if you are a lazy trader, I've tried to segment different types of entry, stops, and exit prices for your ease of reference and decision.

Once you have mastered all the Ichimoku strategies and techniques in this book, you will be confident to apply them in your real trading. A trading strategy is the backbone of any trading system. The sooner you establish a powerful and timeless trade strategy, the sooner you will generate consistent profits.

With all that said, I believe this superb tool provides a complete trading system in terms of finding trade opportunities and appropriate times for entering and exiting trades. While I generally believe in its powerful signals, I would say it's never redundant to combine them with other price analysis tools that you might already have. Just don't try to make things too complicated when you combine different tools. Successful trading should be simple.

Now, before diving into the main part of the book, let's go over two simple and straightforward principles when using the Ichimoku Kinko Hyo toolset presented in this book.

- *Be flexible*

Because Ichimoku Kinko Hyo signals are derived from constantly changing price actions, it requires us to be flexible when using. When you go further in this book, you'll see we tend not to apply some fixed price levels in some strategies. Instead, you'll determine an appropriate price level based on how you read the price movements. For example, if you see a thin Kumo, you might choose a stop-loss above the Kumo. But when you face a thicker Kumo, you'll need to analyze the buy-sell correlation at that point and see whether a stop level at the middle of the Kumo would be more suitable. The financial markets are so volatile, and the more flexible you are in understanding price actions and momentum, the closer you are to generating consistent profits.

- *Expectation over prediction*

Within the Ichimoku, our aim isn't to predict what the market will go next. We just can't make such a prediction. With Ichimoku, we only **expect** where the market may go or cease its move based on what the past price actions are telling. The father of Ichimoku Kinko Hyo insisted in his book about the free state of mind, or trading like having no position. This is where we obtain the best mindset to perform with our trades based on objective and fact-based expectations. By contrast, by trying to predict with some certainty in mind, you shape your mindset the wrong way, which affects your trade negatively. In short, Ichimoku provides reliable trade signals that could be a crucial aid to your trading over the long term, however, there's no guarantee for profit in each trade.

I hope you've got some basic ideas about the Ichimoku Kinko Hyo toolset. Now, if you're ready, let's get started.

CHAPTER 1: ICHIMOKU – A GIFT FROM A LEGEND

The History of Ichimoku Kinko Hyo

Ichimoku Kinko Hyo has an interesting history. The first thing that can make you curious as a trader is that not all Ichimoku concepts are disclosed to the public. Ichimoku concepts present a distinct viewpoint of the market by the investor – Goichi Hosoda. Ichimoku lines and theories cover a wide variety of aspects of market readings and understandings.

Now, let's start with the inventor of this toolset. His name is Goichi Hosoda, and his pen name is Ichimoku Sanjin. He was born in 1898 and was among the top chart analysts in Japan back in the early 90s. Before becoming a renowned chart analyst in his community, he was the sales manager of Miyako newspaper - one of the most famous newspaper companies in Japan at that time. Goichi started analyzing charts and trading when he was 10 years old. He was not only a great analyst but also a successful trader and investor at that time.

After leaving the newspaper company, he started up his research center and devoted most of his time to analyzing the financial markets. During his research and analysis, he combined chart analysis techniques with natural science, philosophy, and mathematics, and finally invented a tool called Ichimoku Kinko Hyo. Before receiving the name as we often call it nowadays, the technique was called "Shinto Tenkan-Sen" when it was first invented in around 1935. In Japanese, "Ichimoku" translates to "one look", "Kynko" means "equilibrium", and "Hyo" means "chart". The name of the tool suggests that the market equilibrium levels can be identified at a glance.

In 1950, he was asked to share his knowledge by three of his friends, and he agreed. This marked the first milestone for his technique to be spread widely a few decades later. Notice that at the time he agreed to reveal his technique, he was already well-known for market analysis and forecast, and he decided to share with those three people only. Of the three, two of whom were the directors of famous securities firms in Japan, and the remaining one has been unknown until today. Can you guess how much they paid him to obtain his secrets of the Ichimoku tool? There's no correct answer, but it was said that the coaching fee was so big that Goichi could build a new house with it. So, it must be a lot of money in exchange for his treasured knowledge.

Although he initially didn't want his secrets to be widely disclosed, he changed his mind and wrote a book about Ichimoku and published it 19 years later. Originally, there were 7 volumes in total, and we can purchase the first four volumes in Tokyo. Regarding the remaining ones, you can buy them at the National Diet Library. The four volumes we can buy in Tokyo are "Ichimoku Kinko Hyo", "Ichimoku Kinko Hyo Complete", "Ichimoku Kinko Hyo Weekly", and "Ichimoku Kinko Hyo - My Best Spectrum".

Now, what we call Ichimoku Kinko Hyo is just a part of his tool/technique. Some people call it an "indicator", but to me, Ichimoku is not just an indicator, but a whole integrated wisdom about the market system. Within the Ichimoku wisdom, the Ichimoku Kinko Hyo indicator is just one of the tools for reading and understanding charts, based on the two sub-groups: _Ichimoku lines_ and _Ichimoku theories_. If you don't understand how Ichimoku Sanjin thinks about the market and its movements, you can't use the Ichimoku Kinko Hyo tool correctly.

Trading philosophy

Before going into the details of Ichimoku elements, let's go over how Ichimoku Sanjin thinks about the market by referring to his own words. Once you've understood the backbone of his analysis method, you can go a long way in understanding the theories and techniques.

The first important phrase that we'll need to remember is to **know the presence of the market**. When we talk about any financial markets, it's always the fight between buyers and sellers. Buyers can take advantage when the price goes up while sellers will get a chance for taking profits as the market goes bearish. During the fight between buyers and sellers, at some point, the equilibrium will collapse, and the market will move toward the winner's direction. In other words, at some point in the market, the power balance will be imbalanced, and the market moves toward the dominant side. You'll need to identify whether buyers or sellers are winning or at least gaining an edge in the market, and that's what he calls *the presence of the market*.

Secondly, Ichimoku Sanjin put a strong emphasis on the **time theory.** He insisted that *time is everything in the market*. If you analyze financial charts long enough, you'll see Ichimoku Kinko Hyo technical tool focuses a lot on *"time"*. As time goes by, market conditions change, which will affect the value and price of an asset. For example, grains may decay as time goes by and their value might be going down, but the value of red wines might rise during the same period. Another example is the price of a coat will go up as winter comes while the prices of refreshing drinks are likely to increase during summer. Depending on the time, the value changes over time, which made him believe that time should be highly focused when analyzing the chart.

Third, Goichi stated, "**simplicity is the truth**". This is also my favorite phrase, and it's also something I truly believe as a professional trader. Complicated things are difficult to manage and hence, are not universal. Instead, simple things are closer to the truth. The market, or the price action, is all about *move* or *don't move*. If it moves, it's either going up or down. You can use as many indicators or tools as possible, but don't forget to look at a chart with simplicity.

The fourth concept of Ichimoku Kinko Hyo that Ichimoku Sanjin emphasized is **be free and surrender**. It means that you should trade without going against the flow. In terms of chart analysis, the most important thing is to identify a (major) change in the market. In the financial markets, one thing for sure is the market movements will change. It might change from an uptrend to a downtrend, or from a trending market to a sideways phase, etc. Also, the changes happen frequently and across every asset or currency pair regardless of how much we analyze beforehand. These changes could result from some fundamental news or any other factors. Therefore, the market environment changes over time, and you need to sense these changes without any biased mindset. That's what he means by **be free and surrender**.

Another philosophy that Goichi mentioned in his original book is **always trade like having no position**. Having a position means you're holding a buy or sell trade. Whereas, having no position means you're out of trading. When you're just watching the market move without any position, you can judge things much more objectively. On the contrary, when you hold a position, you have greed, regret, hope, fear, and other emotions to interfere with your trade analysis and decisions. If you can look at a chart as if you have no position, you can analyze the chart more objectively and are more likely to deal with the changed situations with an appropriate mindset. That's something Ichimoku Sanjin really appreciated in his book.

An appropriate view of Ichimoku

A quick research on the Internet can reveal how Ichimoku Kinko Hyo was applied by many technical traders out there. It's not hard to see some mediocre techniques like *"buy when a gold cross happens"*, or *"buy when the price breaks Kumo upwards"*. Most traders would focus on trade signals released by the Ichimoku lines. To me, this *oversimplified* type of approach isn't reliable for trading purposes. If they use the tool this way, they're not understanding and focusing on the timeless trading philosophies that Goichi Hosoda repeated a lot of times in his original books.

To make a long story short, the *Ichimoku tool* is used to show *the equilibrium of the price within the whole market's momentum*. In essence, *Ichimoku* means *one look*, and it also means *one move ahead*. With the Ichimoku toolset, traders can expect one candlestick movement ahead based on chart and price action analyses.

Ichimoku wasn't originally invented to provide trade signals. Honestly, it does in some cases, and we'll rely on its signals for entering and exit trades in the later chapters of this book. However, before diving into when to use or not to use these signals, we need to explore many related aspects to truly understand the meaning behind the signals.

An interesting thing is that the original book doesn't say about signals as to where to buy or sell, nor does it mention what we often call the "Ichimoku strategy". The book is rather conceptual, almost like a philosophical story of how Ichimoku Sanjin analyzed charts, but the core is to closely investigate the relation between the current and past price levels so that you can expect how the future price will possibly move. That's what makes this tool unique. So, for those who think of Ichimoku as a signal-providing tool, just forget about it from now on.

In the next two chapters, we'll go over every component of the tool, and learn how to combine them to prepare for high-probability trade setups.

CHAPTER 2: THE FIVE MAGICAL LINES, AND MUCH MORE

In this chapter, we'll dig into the five lines which together provide *basic* Ichimoku Kinko Hyo understandings and techniques. We use the word "basic" because these five lines are just the stepping stones within the whole Ichimoku trading secrets. Yet, they are the backbone of some Ichimoku trading strategies, and once we've truly understood the use of these lines, including the meanings they convey and the relationships between them, we'll be in a much better position to understand other Ichimoku concepts and the whole Ichimoku toolset after all.

With that being said, let's move to the first component: Tenkan-Sen.

Tenkan-Sen

Tenkan-Sen, or Conversion Line, is the average value of the lowest and highest prices of an asset over the nearest 9 periods. Below is the formula of the Tenkan-Sen.

Tenkan-Sen = (H9 + L9)/2

Where: H9 is the highest price within the last 9 candlesticks, and L9 is the lowest price during the same period.

Note: The past 9 candlesticks include the current one.

Understanding Tenkan-Sen

Tenkan-Sen is simply a line connecting the mid-prices of successive 9 periods. The mid-price is also called the *market price*, *market level*, or *equilibrium price* as you will see many times in this book. Using a short number of periods for its calculation, Tenkan-Sen shows the short-term price momentum of an asset. Thus, it is often used in combination with other lines within the Ichimoku toolset instead of being used individually. Later in this chapter, we'll learn about the Kijun-Sen and how to combine these two lines to release reliable crossover trade signals.

The equilibrium price

In any financial market, the price rarely goes straight up or down. Instead, it moves in waves, including upward waves and downward waves. By connecting the highs and lows of a wave, you'll get a zone, and the center of the zone is the equilibrium level or price. This is the backbone of Ichimoku strategies which you will find in four out of five Ichimoku lines (the only exception is Chikou Span). Also, the lines which *reflect the market price level* are referred to as Han-ne in Japanese. From now, when I mention about Han-ne, you can understand that it can be any element except the Chikou Span.

By observing changes in the market level, we can have a good overview of the trends in the market. Look at some illustrations below. Do you see that by focusing on the market price level, we can spot the trend easily while avoiding many volatilities that may confuse us?

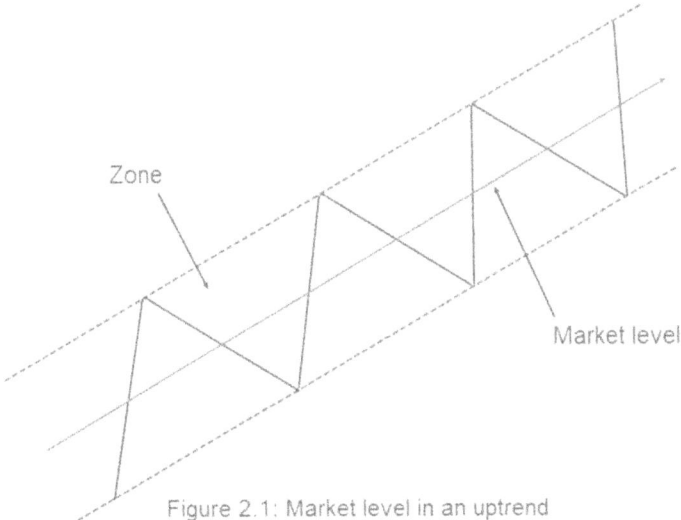

Figure 2.1: Market level in an uptrend

13

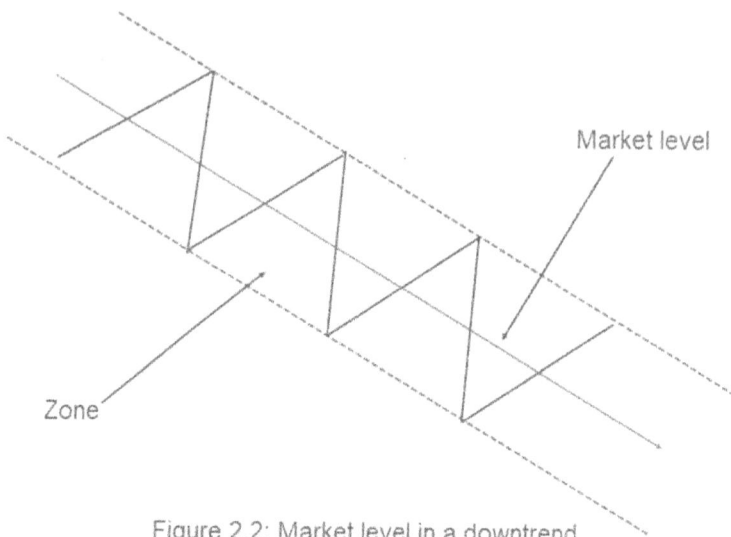

Figure 2.2: Market level in a downtrend

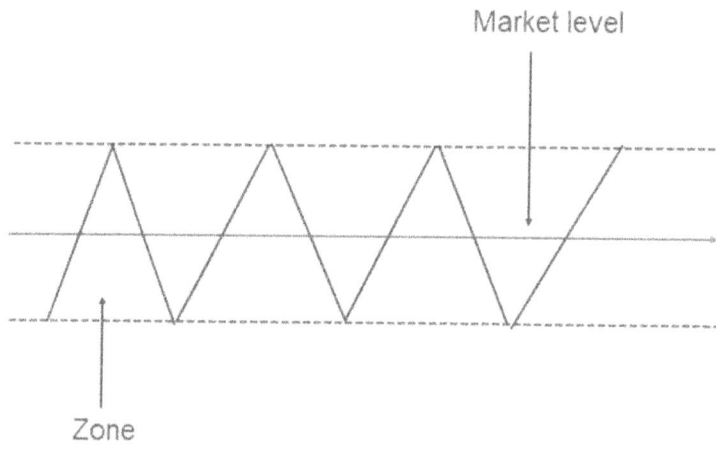

Figure 2.3: Market level in a sideways range

14

The messages of the Tenkan-Sen

The three most important messages the Tenkan-Sen can bring about are "equilibrium", "short-term trend", and "retracement price level".

- First, Tenkan-Sen represents the center of short-term price movements. When the price is at the Tenkan-Sen, this shows that short-term buying and selling powers are temporarily balanced. Put differently, the Tenkan-Sen is the Ichimoku element that shows the equilibrium between short-term buying and selling powers.

- However, the price won't be at the Tenkan-Sen most of the time. If the price is above the Tenkan-Sen, the short-term trend is up, and vice versa. Notice that I use the phrase "short-term", meaning that it can turn into a mid-term or even a long-term trend, or can be collapsed shortly.

- Although the price won't be at the Tenkan-Sen most of the time, it tends to retrace to this line before continuing its move with the dominant trend. In fact, in a strong downtrend, it's common to see the price revisit this short-term price line when retracing. The chart below would be a typical example of this.

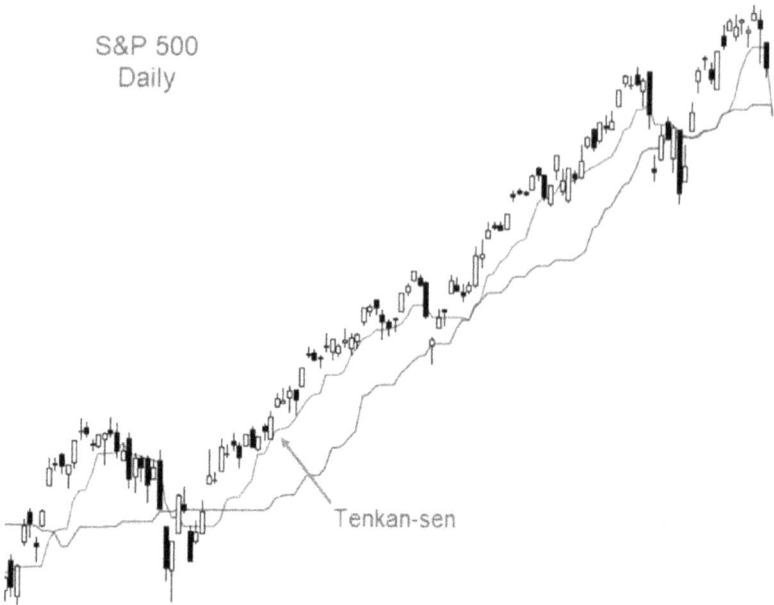

S&P 500
Daily

Tenkan-sen

Figure 2.4: Price retracement to Tenkan-sen

This is the daily chart of the S&P 500 Index between October 2019 and February 2020. The market was in a strong bullish trend, and the price kept remaining above Tenkan-Sen most of the time. Yet, notice the price retraced several times to this line before continuing its upward move. In other words, until the price breaks below the conversion line, any idea of reversal trading should be ignored.

Note that Tenkan-Sen works well in a very strong trend, either an uptrend or a downtrend. During a highly imbalanced market, the retracement price tends to find the Tenkan-Sen or even doesn't touch this line due to the increasing momentum. Yet, at some times during its progression, the price may pierce the Tenkan-Sen and find other components within the Ichimoku toolset such as the Kijun-Sen or the Kumo.

16

Tenkan-Sen provides an important signal to look for during a strong and stable trend. This is where any trader would want to take trades because this is where they can get return the most in a relatively short time.

A strong and stable uptrend is where the price sits above the Tenkan-Sen and goes up along the Tenkan-Sen. Whereas, when the price stably sits below the Tenkan-Sen and goes down along the Tenkan-sen, it is considered a strong downtrend. If the market is going up (or going down) stably, or if the market accelerates the power of a trend, retracements may find the Tenkan-Sen as an ideal level before the dominant trend continues. In other words, by observing whether the retracement is ending at Tenkan-Sen or not, we can assess the strength of the trend.

The best scenario for the price to pull back to Tenkan-Sen is when the price is moving further away from the Tenkan-Sen and widening the distance with the equilibrium price for a longer time than expected. At some point during the period, the dominant side may need to recharge some energy before moving on, and retracements are inevitable.

Kijun-Sen

Kijun-Sen, or Base Line, is the average value of the lowest and highest prices of an asset over the nearest 26 candlesticks. Using a greater number of periods in calculating the line, Kijun-Sen is slower in capturing the price volatility as compared to Tenkan-Sen.

Below is the formula of Kijun-Sen.

Kijun-Sen = (H26 + L26)/2

Where: H26 is the highest price within the last 26 candlesticks, and L26 is the lowest price during the same period.

Note: The past 26 candlesticks include the current one.

Understanding the Kijun-Sen

Kijun-Sen shares some key similarities with Tenkan-Sen, including determining the market price level. The biggest difference is that Kijun-Sen reflects the *mid-term* equilibrium price. The fact that Kijun-Sen is slower than Tenkan-Sen can be seen in the position of these two lines. Take a look at the chart below.

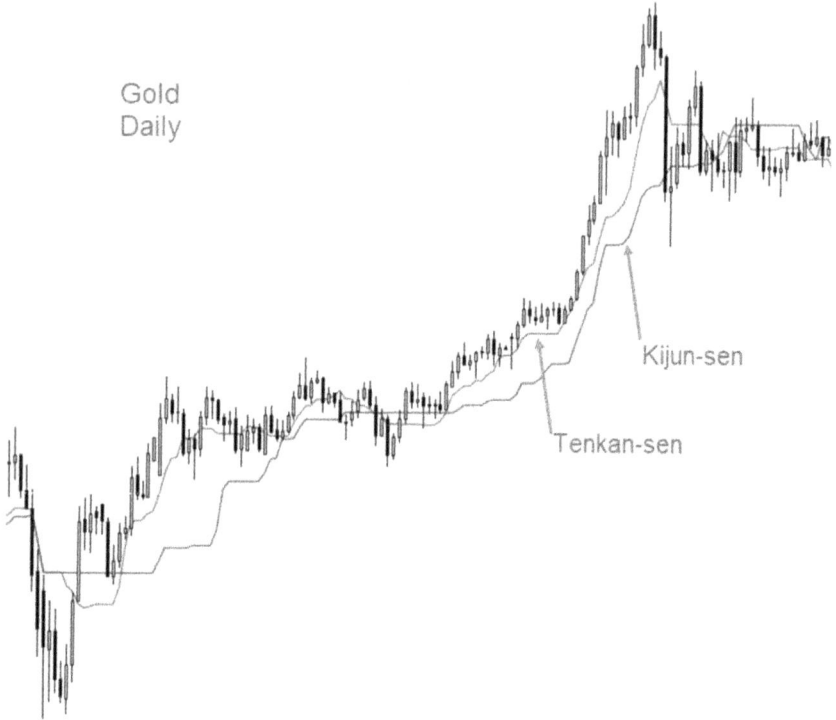

Figure 2.5: Kijun-sen and Tenkan-sen

This is the daily chart of Gold. As can be seen, Tenkan-Sen tends to be closer to the price and is above the Kijun-Sen in a stable uptrend. In general, when we move from the left to the right, we'll have the price, Tenkan-Sen, and Kijun-Sen. An inverse order will apply in a (strong) downtrend where the Tenkan-Sen is below the Kijun-Sen, and both lines are above the price most of the time.

18

Note: Ichimoku lines should be recognized at a glance as its name suggests. Considering Tenkan-Sen is closer to the price most of the time in a trending market, we can easily identify this short-term equilibrium line without having to rely on the color of the line. Meanwhile, Kijun-Sen is the next line the price can touch if it crosses through Tenkan-Sen. Some newbie traders may be confused about differentiating these two lines. Now, with this simple tip, you can easily avoid this confusion from the beginning.

The messages of the Kijun-Sen

- *Mid-term market level & direction of the mid-term trend*

The first point can easily be seen from its formula where we take the mid-prices of successive 26 periods in plotting the line.

Moreover, as mentioned, the market level is the standard price for a certain time period. Hence, the direction of the Kijun-Sen is also the direction of the mid-term trend. In an uptrend, the market price will go up, and vice versa. Take a look at the chart below.

Figure 2.6: Kijun-sen

When the price is right at the Kijun-Sen, it indicates that the buying and selling powers are equally balanced over the mid-term. Put differently, the Kijun-Sen

19

value shows the equilibrium point between the buying and selling powers over the mid-term. For the past 26 candlesticks, there was a downtrend. The price moved from the 26-day high to the 26-day low and then corrected to the Kijun-Sen level. In this case, the Kijun-Sen value represents the 50% retracement of the price. If the price is resisted by the Kijun-Sen, chances are that the overall trend may resume soon. Otherwise, we should watch out for more price reactions to see whether the trend has reversed.

In this example, the current price level is located above the Kijun-Sen, hence we can assume that buyers are gaining a mid-term advantage.

- *Price retracement target over mid-term*

If the trend isn't very strong, the price can be bounced off of Tenkan-Sen. The next target after the break will be Kijun-Sen. In some cases, the Kijun-Sen is an ideal destination for price retracement. It should be noted that although the short-term powers have temporarily reversed, the mid and long-term powers are still intact as long as the price cannot break the Kijun-Sen. If you're having a buy position, a retracement at Kijun-Sen suggests that although the short-term trend temporarily turns bearish, the battle in the mid-term is still under buyers' control. On the other hand, if you're having a sell position, a pullback at Kijun-Sen indicates the short-term trend temporarily becomes bullish, but sellers' power remains intact over the mid-term.

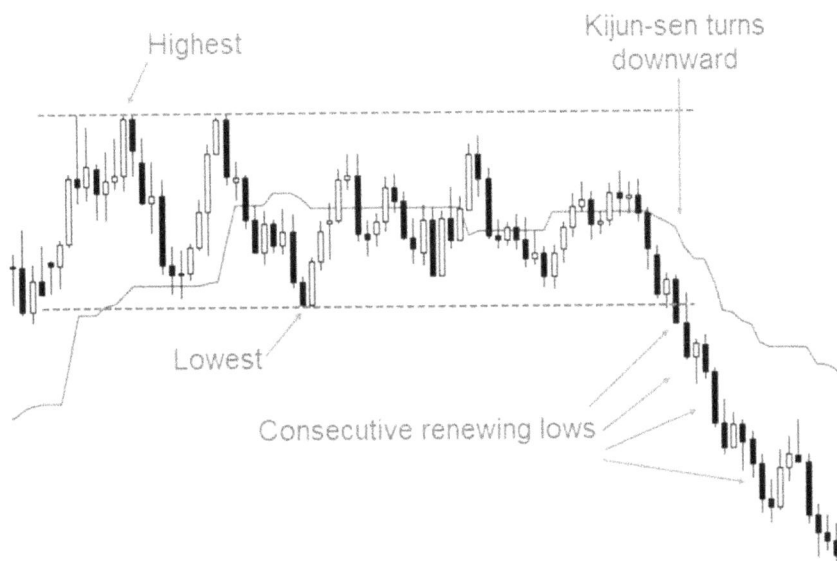

Figure 2.7: The end of a consolidation

Each of the five lines of the Ichimoku Kinko Hyo toolset is great for analyzing the market. Look at the chart above with the Kijun-Sen in place. When the market is in a consolidation period, the Kijun-Sen tends to become flat. This is the unique characteristic of the Han-ne in general.

As long as the highest and lowest prices remain unchanged, the Han-ne lines keep their horizontal direction. In other words, the fact that the Kijun-Sen being flat for a relatively long time is a sign of the continuing consolidation. Sooner or later, the Kijun-Sen will change its direction, either upward or downward. That's when it can show a potential range breakout by renewing the recent high or low. By looking at the Kijun-Sen, you can get what the market wants to tell over the mid-term.

Gold Cross and Death Cross (Kinko Hyo Cross)

This is probably the most important point when we talk about the two Ichimoku lines we've just discussed. Although there are some whipsaws when it comes to the crossover, it opens many good trading opportunities. Don't worry, I'm here to help you make the best use of this crossover taking a number of filters into account. We'll go into detail about it in Chapter 4. But first, let's go over some basic concepts of the cross.

Basically, when Tenkan-Sen crosses above Kijun-Sen, this is a **gold cross** and signals that the short-to-mid-term price movement is generally upward. Whereas, when Tenkan-Sen crosses below Kijun-Sen, this is a **death cross** and we should pay more attention to sell opportunities. We've been familiar with "buy on a gold cross" and "sell on a death cross". However, this is a very dangerous idea of trading with crosses, which may blow up your trading account very quickly.

Now, to make things clearer, this is just a basic definition of the cross between the two lines, and won't be correct in some cases. To avoid the whipsaws I just mentioned, we need to put the cross in a favorable trading context by analyzing the correlation between Ichimoku elements, reading the price action carefully, and understanding market momentums to best determine whether the crossover provides a reliable trade signal or not. Note that Kijun-Sen indicates a base or a reference trend direction of the market. A cross between the conversion line (Tenkan-Sen) and the reference line (Kijun-Sen) indicates where a downtrend turns into an uptrend or vice versa. That's why Tenkan-Sen is called a *conversion line* and Kijun-Sen is called a *base line*.

Let's look at the diagram below.

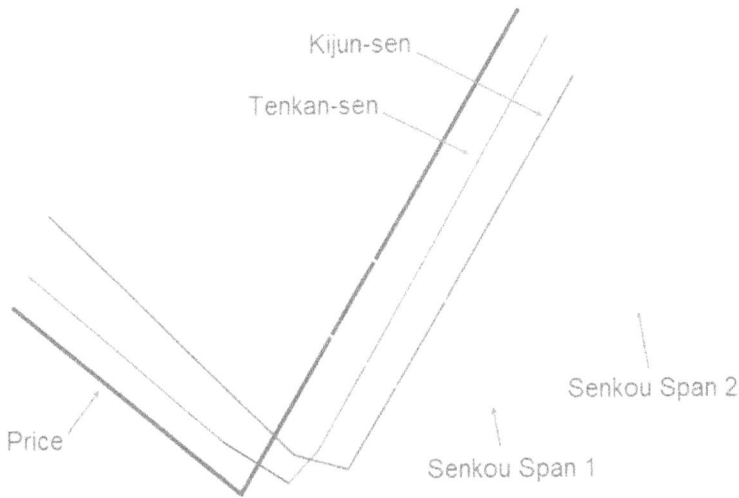

Figure 2.8: Ichimoku basic diagram

The figure above is an ideal Ichimoku Kinko Hyo diagram. A price movement is simplified in the bold line to show how each line in the Ichimoku Kinko Hyo lines up. This diagram is used to create a hypothetical price change that transforms from a downtrend to an uptrend.

Looking at the diagram where the price is stably going down, you will notice that all the lines in the Ichimoku Kinko Hyo are going down in parallel. In contrast, during a stable bullish trend, each line is going up in parallel. Furthermore, if the lines are not moving in parallel, this is when the trend is getting weaker. You can grasp this basic price momentum just by looking at the change of spacing between lines. When the market repeatedly goes up (or down), Kinko Hyo crosses become excellent trading signals.

Now, let's turn our attention to fake crosses that we should avoid in the market.

Fake crosses

Any technical strategy has its drawbacks, and Kinko Hyo Cross is not an exception. Mastering crossover trading entails understanding when the fakes occur, the reasons behind them, and how to avoid them. Within the Ichimoku

Kinko Hyo context, false crosses are more likely to happen when the market is in a *consolidation period*, or *sideways range*.

When the market is consolidating, it doesn't make sense to say "buy on a gold cross" or "sell on a death cross". In other words, a sideways range is an ideal condition for fake crosses to occur.

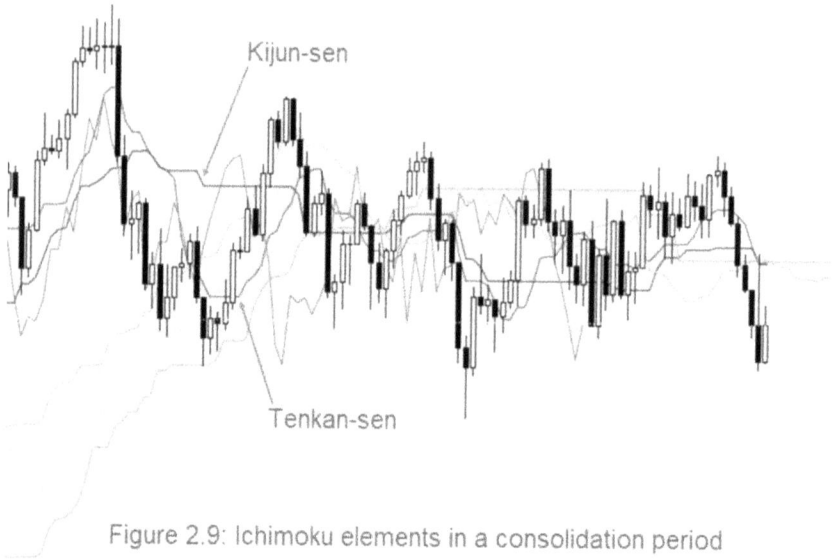

Figure 2.9: Ichimoku elements in a consolidation period

This chart illustrates how each line of the Ichimoku Kinko Hyo moves as the market loses its volatility. The lines are constantly crossing back and forth without signifying a clear direction. Notice the Kijun-Sen remains flat in some periods within the whole picture. Tenkan-Sen does cross above and below Kijun-Sen but changes its direction very quickly after the cross. These lines above look like a mess which can easily cause any trade to hit the stop-loss. In short, in the case of a consolidation period, most Kinko Hyo crosses have little to no meaning.

You can determine the difference between a reliable trend and a weak trend by observing how the movement of each line changes. The determination of a sideways range becomes quite easy after we see consecutive line crosses. However, the beginning of a range is relatively difficult to capture, and this is where you need to pay close attention to the slope and the speed of changing the direction of both lines to assess the potential of a sideways range.

Now, we've understood that a sideways range won't be a good condition to trade the crosses. Yet, our strategy with golden crosses and death crosses later in this book is closely connected with this period in the market. This is one interesting thing to expect in the first trading method in this book.

Reliable Death Cross and Gold Cross

Now that we've discussed some typical signals of both reliable crosses and fake crosses, let's now combine them into some necessary conditions of a reliable Kinko Hyo gold cross.

- Kijun-Sen should be sloping up. If not, it should point upwards soon after the gold cross occurs.
- The Kijun-Sen has been going up for some time since the market marked the lowest price.
- The price may temporarily go below the Kijun-Sen immediately after the gold cross, but it should go up soon.
- Price and Tenkan-Sen go up steadily. Even if there can be a temporary retracement, it only lasts for a short period, and the price should be pushed back again without crossing Kijun-Sen downwards.
- Kijun-Sen shouldn't be flat for long.

Following these conditions will increase your chance of determining a reliable gold cross while capturing a large portion of profits within a trending move.

On the other hand, below is the checklist for a potentially fake gold cross. In these cases, you might want to consider closing the buy position.

- Kijun-Sen goes horizontally for a long time.
- Kijun-Sen turns downwards.
- Price and Tenkan-Sen begin to go down towards the Kijun-Sen.

Figure 2.10: Fake gold cross

The chart above shows a gold cross example. We can see both Tenkan-Sen and Kijun-Sen turn upward soon after the gold cross. The short-term bull trend is indicated by two long bullish candlesticks. However, a fake cross is characterized by a change in the direction of the lines. After forming a top, the market quickly goes all the way down, causing the Tenkan-Sen to cross below Kijun-Sen quite strongly. Thus, in this example, both the gold cross and the death cross occur in a short span of time, and the gold cross is clearly a fake one.

Now, let's move on to the Kinko Hyo death cross. Basically, it's completely opposite to the gold cross. First, make sure to go over some conditions below for a reliable death cross.

- Kijun-Sen should be sloping down. If not, it should point downward soon after the death cross occurs.
- The Kijun-Sen has been going down for some time since the market marked the highest price.
- The price may temporarily go above the Kijun-Sen immediately after the death cross, but it should go down soon.

26

- Price and Tenkan-Sen go down steadily. Even if there can be a temporary retracement, it only lasts for a short period, and the price should be pushed back again without crossing Kijun-Sen upwards.
- Kijun-Sen shouldn't be horizontal for long.

On the other hand, below is the checklist for a potentially fake death cross. In these cases, you might want to consider closing the sell position.

- Kijun-Sen goes horizontally for a long time.
- Kijun-Sen turns upwards.
- Price and Tenkan-Sen begin to go up towards the Kijun-Sen.

The first part of the Kinko Hyo gold cross and death cross ends here. Until now, we've understood the danger of trading crossovers during a consolidation period as well as signals of a potential gold cross or death cross. It seems simple, but mastering these ideas can save you tons of hard-earned money in trading. The main idea in trading gold and death crosses is you should observe carefully what the price action and Ichimoku lines are telling, and avoid jumping the gun.

Understanding these lines goes hand in hand with understanding price trends in the market. Later in this book, I'll share how to make use of a sideways market to flow with the next trending market and capture a large movement of the price.

Now, let's shift our attention to the third component of the Ichimoku five-line toolset – Chikou Span.

Chikou Span

Now, let's move on to the only line which is not a Han-ne line – the Chiko Span (lagging Span). Chiko means "delay" in Japanese, and it's simply the 26-period delayed line of the current close price. In other words, you take the current close price, move it to 26 candlesticks before, and that's where Chiko Span is. In many cases, the Chikou Span is used as a momentum indicator and as a confirmation tool in conjunction with the other elements of the Ichimoku toolset.

On a trading chart, Chikou Span is typically the line that goes behind the price and is furthest from the current price.

<u>The Formula of the Chikou Span</u>

CS= Current close price plotted 26 periods backward.

Where: CS = Chikou Span

Chikou Span is a unique line in the Ichimoku context because it doesn't reflect the mid-price level in any period. The most important purpose of this component is to compare the current price with that of 26 periods ago.

Now, I bet you are wondering "why do we need to make this comparison?" To make a long story short, looking at the Chikou Span, you can instantly understand how the market has been performing for the last 26 periods based on where the current price is at. The Chikou span helps traders to visualize the latest trend in the market and gauge potential trend reversals.

In the next chapter, we will learn that 26 is one of the base numbers in Ichimoku Kinko Hyo - the psychological number in terms of how long a trader tends to hold their positions. If traders are making profits on their trades, they tend to close their positions after around 9, 26, or 52 periods. Or, when they're not making profits due to a persisting consolidation, they also tend to close their positions after 26 periods. Within the Ichimoku Kinko Hyo context, a trend is deemed to be upward when the Chikou span is above the price, and downward when the indicator is below the price. Many traders watch for the Chikou span to cross a prior price level as a signal for a potential trend change.

If the Chikou span crosses up through the price, this could signal the beginning of an uptrend. The price will have already started to move higher and the price advance may continue. Similarly, if the Chikou drops below the price (after being separated for some time), that could indicate that the price has started to fall and could be continuing its downward trend.

However, these ideas won't be applicable when the price is crossing back and forth with the Chikou line. Like some other technical tools, Chikou Span doesn't work well in a consolidation phase. This range might just be a rest time for the dominant side, and the trend might be resuming soon after one side has recharged enough energy to drive the price in the market.

Given the above, if the Chikou span crosses the price *after a certain distance between them* for some time, this might trigger a trend reversal.

Let's look at a real chart below.

Figure 2.11: Chikou Span

This is the daily chart of EUR/USD. I've hidden other lines and only left the Chikou Span on the chart so that we can better view the relationship between the line and the price. As mentioned, the lagging line is 26-period behind the actual price levels. To the top left of the chart, the Chikou line was continuously interacting with the candlesticks. This indicated the market was in a consolidation period, and neither buyers nor sellers were winning or gaining an advantage in the market.

However, things changed when the Chikou Span broke the candlesticks decisively to the downside. This indicated the sellers started to dominate the game. Notice after the break, the lagging line couldn't return to touch the candlestick, and a strong downtrend was initiated. It wasn't until the Chikou Span cross the price gain that the market entered into an official sideways period. In this ideal example, the Chikou Span cross can provide a take-profit suggestion as well. Generally, the Chikou Span's break can be an early signal of a downtrend or uptrend if this is a decisive break and comes after a long consolidation period.

In conclusion, Chiko Span is merely a line that's delayed 26 periods before, but it tells you how sellers and buyers have been performing during that period so that you can expect the next trend after the sideways phase. Note that 26 is one of the possible numbers of the period that traders can bare to hold their positions.

This is a fairly straightforward section, and I hope you've grasped fully what I conveyed so far. In the next part, we'll go over two components in the Ichimoku toolset which together form the last (and strongest) layer of defense for the current trend.

Ichimoku Cloud

This chapter will focus on the Kumo (or "cloud") which is composed of two components: Senkou Span A (or "Senkou Span 1", "Leading Span A", "Leading Span 1") and Senkou Span B (or "Senkou Span 2", "Leading Span B", "Leading Span 2"). The cloud plays as a support or resistance level and is plotted 26 periods into the future. It's considered the last defense for the current dominant trend. When the price breaks the Kumo to the upside or downside after a long trending move, the trend might be reversing.

In the previous sections, we've learned about the short-term and mid-term market prices with Tenkan-Sen and Kijun-Sen. In this section, we'll begin with the Senkou Span B – a reflection of the long-term market price.

Senkou Span B

Senkou Span B is one of five elements of the Ichimoku Cloud indicator. Being plotted 26 periods into the future, Senkou Span B provides a hint of where support and resistance may come next.

Below is the formula of the Senkou Span B.

Senkou Span B = (H52 + L52)/2

Where: H52 is the highest price within the last 52 candlesticks, and L52 is the lowest price within the last 52 candlesticks.

Note: The past 52 candlesticks include the current one.

If Senkou Span B is the upper line of the cloud, the trend is generally bearish. Short-term prices (Span A – we'll learn about it in the next section) have fallen below the longer-term price midpoint (Span B).

When Senkou Span B is the lower line of the cloud, the trend is generally bullish since the shorter-term midpoint price (Span A) is moving above the longer-term midpoint price (Span B).

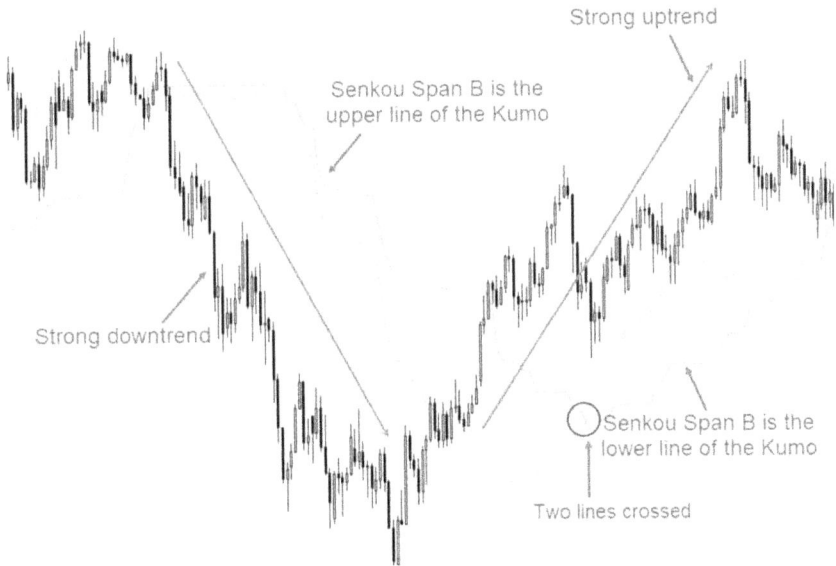

Figure 2.12: Ichimoku Cloud

In this USD/JPY daily chart, there are two opposite trends. In the first half of the chart, the trend is bearish, and the Senkou Span B is the upper line of the

Kumo throughout this strong trend. In the second half of the chart, the trend is up, and Senkou Span B plays as the lower boundary of the Kumo during the majority of this uptrend. Notice the intersection between the two lines of Kumo signals an official trend change in this example. Also, it should be noted that the Kumo is projected 26 candlesticks forward, hence at the time of the cross, we are at 26 candlesticks backward – a good price to capture the majority of the trend.

Understanding Senkou (Leading) Span B

Senkou Span B shares a common characteristic with Tenkan-Sen and Kijun-Sen in the calculation formula. In other words, this line also reflects the equilibrium price in the market. It's where the price tends to come back after a long trending move. However, there are two key differences between Senkou Span B and the other two. First, using the 52 periods as a reference, this line reflects the long-term market price (compared to short-term and mid-term indications in Tenkan-Sen and Kijun-Sen). Second, the Senkou Span B, like Senkou Span A, is projected for 26 periods in the future.

Now, you might be asking "why do we need to plot 26 periods ahead?". Let's look at a chart example to find the answer to this question as well as to understand the secrets behind the formation of the Senkou Span B.

Figure 2.13: Senkou Span 2

As I mentioned earlier, Senko Span 2 shows the equilibrium point of the longer time span as compared to Tenkan-Sen and Kijun-Sen. When the price breaks the Senko span 2, it breaks the whole Kumo.

This is a daily chart of Gold. The vertical line on the left is on Feb 26th, and the vertical line to the right of the chart is on April 01st. If you calculate the number of days between Feb 26th and April 01st, it's exactly 52 trading days. The Senko Span 2 is at the lower edge of the Kumo, the middle price of the range between the highest price of 1262.51 and the lowest price of 1047.89.

Now, let's say the market that's been going up for the past 52 days starts to go down with *the same speed or momentum*. Then, from the highest price level, how many days can we expect the market may take to come back to the middle price? Simply, if the market takes 52 days to go up from the lowest to the highest price in the market, it typically takes another 52 days to go bearish from the highest price to the lowest price level. Hence, to retrace back to the middle price, the market generally needs 26 days, right? Again, this is what we can expect only because the ups and downs in the market cannot be forecast with

33

100% certainty. We can only infer from what the market has performed with the assumption that the momentum remains unchanged.

Senko Span 2 helps us to forecast where the equilibrium price can be in a long-time span. That's the reason why it's forwarded 26 candles ahead. With Senkou Span 2, we focus on the concept of "expectation" instead of "prediction". Plotting the Kumo doesn't serve to predict the future (no one can do that). The true meaning behind the use of Senkou Span B (and Senkou Span A as well) is to monitor and compare if the current price action is strong or weak compared to past price behaviors. This drives us to the next concept in connection with the Senkou Span B – the forecast line.

The forecast line connects the price (ideally a top or bottom) with the current Senkou Span B level.

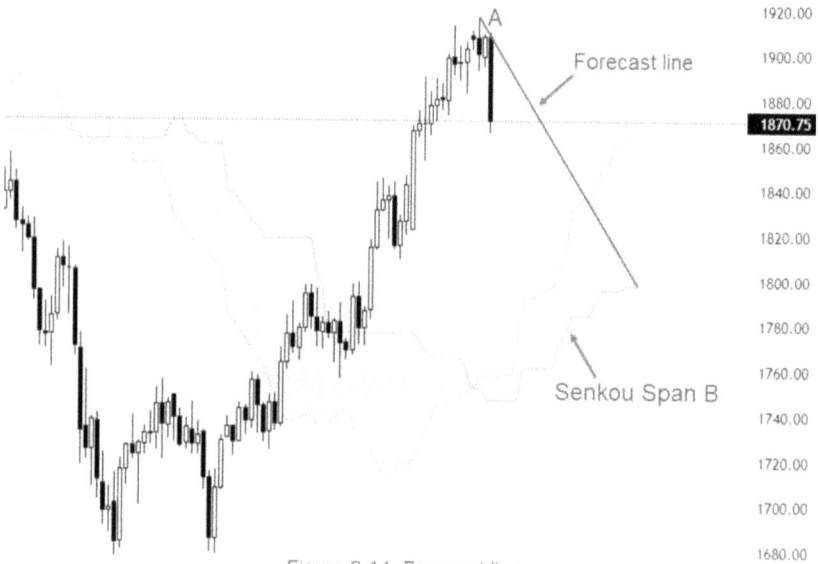

Figure 2.14: Forecast line

In this chart example, the forecast line is a reference line so that we can compare the retracement momentum in the market. Let's assume A is the swing high in this uptrend, and the market is going into a retracement phase. If the next candlesticks within the pullback phase remain mostly above the forecast line, the retracement momentum is generally not strong enough, and the trend might resume soon. On the other hand, if the price remains mostly under the reference line, we might expect a deeper retracement, and even consider entering a pullback trade. In the second Ichimoku strategy later in this book, I'll show how to combine the forecast line with a powerful technique in identifying a retracement trade opportunity.

The power of Senkou Span B lies in the **reference** purpose. Without any reference, you cannot know what's right and what's wrong. Let's say you are a salesperson in a company and made $20,000 in sales this month. If you don't know the standard reference or KPI, you won't be able to tell if your result is good enough within the company, correct? On the other hand, if you have the average sales figure within the department, and your figure turns out to be beyond that average, then you can say you have an acceptable result. By contrast, no matter how big the sales you've made within the month are, if the result is below the average, that means your result is relatively bad.

When you have a standard reference, you'll know whether the performance is good or bad, and also how good or how bad it is. That's what Ichimoku Kinko Hyo wants to look at. It shows the standard reference point of the market to bring you a better view of the market. When the price is going up, buyers never feel worried about it because they are basically on profit, and as more buyers come into the market, it keeps going up. However, at some point, the market will retrace. The question is where or when the buyers should hold their positions during a trending market. This is the hardest part because if you keep holding your position after the trend reverse or even goes beyond where you bought, then your hard-earned profit will turn into a loss. On the other hand, if you close the position too early, you'll lose the chance of maximizing profits, which in turn might affect your psychological state.

So, until now you might have known the true meaning behind the use of Senko Span B. It actually shows the psychological spot in the market. Let's say the market marks the highest, but it's just going slightly down for the next couple of days. This might cause some buyers to worry due to the downward price action. But if you use Senkou Span 2 and the forecast line drawn correspondingly, you can avoid such unnecessary worry.

Now, let's move to the second component of the Kumo – the Senkou Span A.

<u>Senkou Span A</u>

Senkou Span A is the last element of the Ichimoku tool that we discuss in this chapter. It is used to measure the price momentum and can provide trade ideas based on support and resistance levels. It works in close combination with the Senkou Span B to form the Kumo cloud.

Like Senkou Span B, this line's calculation is plotted 26 periods into the future, indicating where key levels may form down the road.

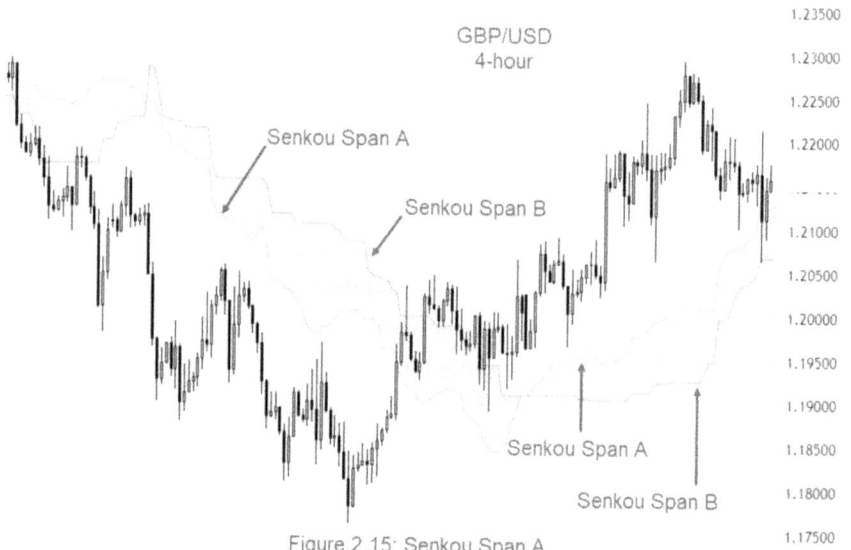

Figure 2.15: Senkou Span A

Below is the formula of the Senkou Span A.

Senkou Span A = (Tenkan-Sen + Kijun-Sen)/2

Where:

H9 and H26 are the highest price levels within the last 9 and 26 candlesticks respectively, and L9 and L26 are the lowest price levels within the last 9 and 26 candlesticks respectively.

As we learn in the previous section, the Senkou Span B line is considered to be the long-term market price because it is calculated using 52 periods of data. Senkou Span A, on the other hand, uses data for the last 26 periods and 9 periods, hence it reacts quicker to price changes. Taking the two lines into consideration, the Senkou Span A is always closer to the price in a trending market as can be seen in the figure above.

In a trending market, moving from the left to the right, we'll have the following typical order: Chikou Span, candlestick, Tenkan-Sen, Kijun-Sen, Senkou Span A, and Senkou Span B. The four elements after the candlestick pattern are the Han-ne lines and play as layers of defense for the prevailing trend. Now, when the price violates the Kumo by crossing Senko Span A, this indicates the price might be in a dangerous zone. In other words, we should be careful with our trade position when the price enters the Kumo territory.

A crossover between Span A and Span B can signal a trend change. When Senkou Span A crosses above Senkou Span B, an uptrend or a correction might be starting. When Senkou Span A crosses below Senkou Span B, this may indicate the start of a downtrend or correction.

When the price is above Span A and/or Span B, these lines may act to support and present possible buying areas. In contrast, when the price is below Span A and/or Span B, these lines may act as resistance, providing possible areas to go short. Look at the example below.

Figure 2.16: Kumo break

This is a daily chart of USD/JPY. If you look at the price action, it's been on a stable bull trend most of the time. However, after forming the top during the period, the price made a retracement, breaking the Senko Span 1 downwards and going into the Kumo.

If you have a buy position and are still holding it, you don't have to worry about closing your position as long as the price remains above the Senko Span A. However, when the price breaks below the Senkou Span A and enters the Kumo, it's when you should watch out for the market. There is a possibility that the market could break the whole Kumo downwards. On this chart, the price first went into Kumo but it didn't break Kumo right away. After some up and down movements without breaking out of the Kumo, the price makes another strong bearish move and breaks the Senkou Span B – the last defense of the trend – quite easily. This is when you should consider closing your buy position.

When we see a candlestick inside Kumo, we should stay out of trading because it could go either direction. In general, I prefer to trade after the price breaks Kumo upwards or downwards. Each time we look at Kumo, let's imagine the price as an airplane and Kumo as a storm. When the airplane is way above or below the storm, the weather is beautiful with all the sunshine and the flight is going well. On the other hand, the airplane never wants to enter any storms. Correct? Things are similar in trading.

In this case, within the Kumo storm, the wind was strong with lots of rain and thunders. The flight got very unstable and tried its best to exit as soon as possible. This explains why the price broke the Senkou Span B right the first time it touched the line. The price entering the Kumo can be very challenging in trading, and this is the reason why I avoid trading in such an unstable condition.

Putting all together

Until now, we've learned five components in the Ichimoku toolset. These components are the cornerstone of many trading strategies within the Ichimoku context. I call them the first half of the Ichimoku arsenal.

Now, let's put all these elements together and read the chart based on the signals they give. You'll see that these signals can provide a lot of insights into price action. Take a look at the chart below.

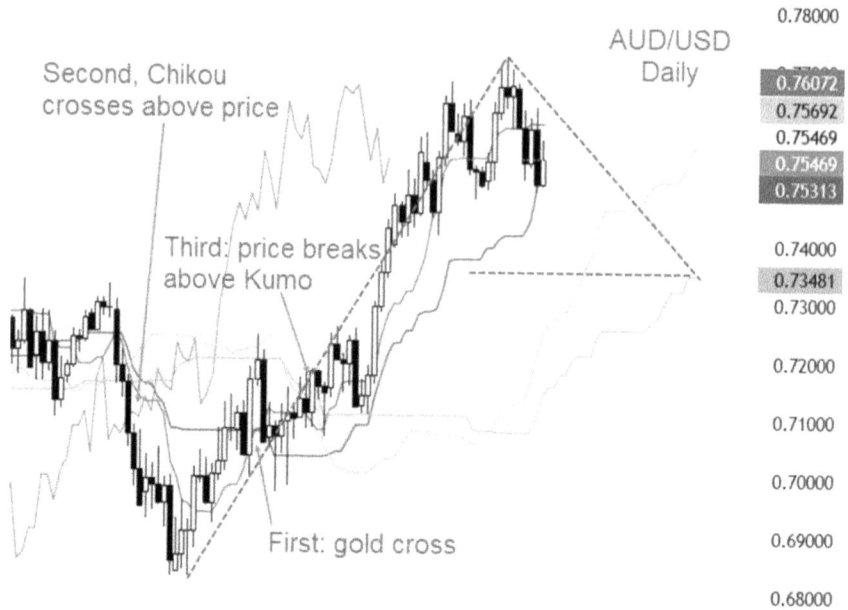

Second, Chikou
crosses above price

AUD/USD
Daily

0.78000

0.76072
0.75692
0.75469
0.75469
0.75313

Third: price breaks
above Kumo

0.74000

0.73481

0.73000

0.72000

0.71000

0.70000

First: gold cross

0.69000

0.68000

Figure 2.17: Analyze a gold cross

In this chart, we have a strong bull trend in place. When a bull trend starts, the Tenkan-Sen typically crosses Kijun-Sen to the upside (gold cross), then Chiko Span crosses the candlestick upward, then finally, the price breaks Kumo upwards. This is called Sanyaku Kouten in Japanese, meaning three positive signals. This is the typical sign of a beginning bull trend.

When the price starts to go up, the first thing to look at is Tenkan-Sen. When the momentum is strong as shown in this example, the price tends to be supported by the Tenkan-Sen.

The next support line will be Kijun-Sen. As long as the market is above Kijun-Sen, you don't need to worry about closing the position, just keep holding it at least until the price hits the Kijun-Sen. Or, if you don't have any position yet, wait until the price finds support at the Tenkan-Sen or Kijun-Sen and consider placing a trade in the direction of the dominant trend.

The next level of support is the Kumo. If you look at the recent candlesticks, they're staying at the Kijun-Sen. Once the price isn't supported by the Kijun-

Sen, it might be hitting Kumo next. Once the price breaks the Senko Span A downwards, it goes into a storm, where the market can be unstable. The price may go way down to Senko Span 2, or it could be in a range with some volatility. As I mentioned before, if the price enters into Kumo, it's better to stay away from trading at least until the price breaks Kumo in either direction.

Still, on the chart above, I've plotted two diagonal lines. The upward line connects the lowest and highest price level during the last 52 periods – they're the data to calculate the Senkou Span 2. The downward line connects the highest high during the last 52 periods with the latest Senkou Span 2 – this is the forecast line.

Based on what I said earlier about Senko Span 2, what can you conclude about the price momentum on the chart?

Let's look at the last seven candlesticks in the retracement phase. By comparing the forecast line with the price action, you can see that the price action remains below this line, meaning that the current bearish momentum is relatively stronger, or the market sentiment is relatively sell-biased. In this case, if the price goes straight down to the horizontal line drawn from the current Senko Span 2 and breaks it downwards in less than 26 periods calculated from the highest price, chances are that the retracement phase might continue and the bull trend is in danger. On the contrary, if the price is supported by the Senko Span 1, then the bull trend might continue afterward.

In case the price forms another high, then we'll take that high and update the new forecast line so that you can assess the momentum of the market at that time. This is basically how I use Ichimoku Kinko Hyo to grasp some initial ideas of the price action, and this has been working very well, especially on the daily timeframe or above. Of course, you can use it on the 1-hour timeframe or below, however, from my experience, the longer timeframe works the best with this toolset.

CHAPTER 3: ADVANCED ICHIMOKU CONCEPTS

In this chapter, we'll go into detail about the most overlooked part within the Ichimoku context. Most books and courses out there only focus on the five lines we've just learned about. In fact, one of the original Ichimoku volumes emphasizes the ***three theories*** which were cultivated through years of research and summary by Goichi Hosoda. These include the *time theory*, *wave theory*, and *price theory*, providing both the momentum of the price as well as potential price reversal points and price targets.

These theories reflect a distinct view of the financial market by Goichi Hosoda that we cannot witness anywhere else. Like any other techniques and theories in trading, you'll need to practice with it a lot and observe as many charts as possible to grasp the market insights and apply them successfully in trading.

The next section will bring you some "aha" moments in investigating the time theory. Now, if you're ready, let's get started.

Time Theory

One thing I truly believe is, whenever you use any indicator, you have to understand the core value in it. It's like what purpose it serves, why it's formed, and what makes it different from others (the uniqueness). You'll need to understand the message the indicator conveys.

One of the best ways to grasp the idea behind the use of any indicator is through its calculation. As we all know, when working with the five lines within the Ichimoku Kinko Hyo context, nearly every element is closely connected with the base number, or "Kihon Suchi" in Japanese. These base numbers are 9, 17, and 26, etc. From these three numbers, we have a ten-number string as follows:

9, 17, 26, 33, 42, 65, 76, 129, 172, 257

From the number sequence above, there are some interrelations between numbers, and all numbers are derived from basic numbers in some ways.

For example, 9 + 17 = 26; 26+17 − 1 = 42; 33+9 = 42; 33 x 2 − 1 = 65; 42 + 33 -1 = 76; 65 x 2 − 1 = 129; 129 + 42 - 1 = 172, etc.

Within the Ichimoku context, these numbers reflect typical cycles of the market. Within the trading context, we'll focus on smaller periods such as 17, 26, 33, or 42. These periods are more likely to happen and are easier to recognize *at a glance.*

A quick look at a financial chart can reveal many cycles with 9 candles or 26 candles in between. For example, if the bull trend lasts for 9 candlesticks, then a successive bear trend may remain for 9 bars as well. Or, if it takes 26 days to go bearish and the price marks the lowest, then from this price level, it may take another 26 days to come back to the next swing high. This law of cycle is called **the time theory** and it's one of the three theories in the Ichimoku Kinko Hyo context that we'll learn in this chapter. The time theory focuses on the horizontal axis in the chart. Once you've mastered the time theory, you can be in a much better position to watch out for price reversals in the market. Ichimoku Sanjin once stated that *"Time is everything in the market"*.

Time is considered the most important part of the three theories because the price in the market is strongly affected by time. Within the Ichimoku context, we have one crucial *"ruler"* that helps us to measure time: Kihon Suchi. Kihon Suchi numbers show the time period (measured by the number of candlesticks) that the market might reverse, or until when a particular trend will persist.

"Ruler" is very important. Imagine when you try to design and build a chair from wood with your friends, you cannot just cut the wood by your instinct because there may be some differences of opinions among people, which might end up in the failure to connect the parts together. However, when you have a ruler, you can have the common sense as to where exactly the wood needs to be cut in as specific as millimeters, which helps you to cut the wood with the exact length and build those parts perfectly eventually.

The sample principle applies in trading. When you look at a chart with your friend, where the trend starts and ends can be different from one another. You might think the trend starts from this candlestick, but your friend might disagree with you. This is because traders have their own rulers, and they might not see what you see. This boils down to different ways of interpreting the market movements among traders, and that isn't something too hard to understand. To avoid that confusion, Ichimoku gives us the ruler called Kihon Suchi which is aligned with the horizontal time axis. Look at the illustration below.

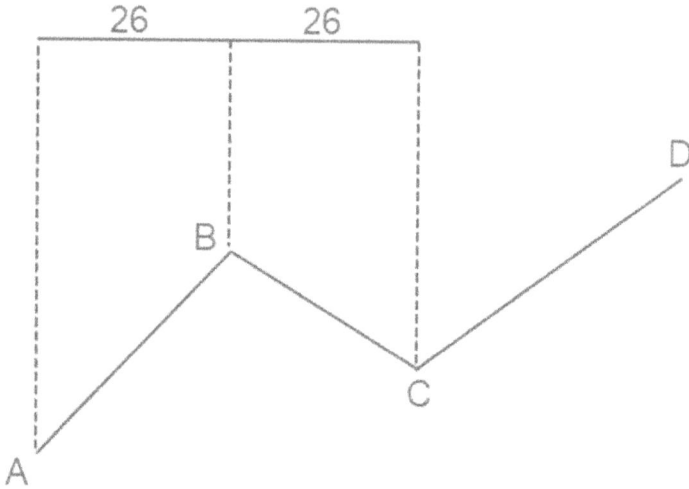

Figure 3-1: Kihon Suchi time cycle

Let's say we have a market formation like this. You see that B is the nearest swing high in place. When you go 26 candlesticks backward from point B, you find point A. In this case, you can say that the market from A to B is on the 26-day cycle, or on one of Kihon Suchi's cycles. Then, when you measure the distance from B to C, it might also be a 26-period or a similar cycle. Similarly, from C to D, it might also be another cycle of the same size. This is the first concept in the time principle – the Kihon Suchi cycle.

Next, there's another type of ruler in Ichimoku Kinko Hyo which is called "Taito Suchi" in Japanese, which is directly translated as "equal numbers". Taito Suchi shares a lot of similarities with Kihon Suchi, but there is one major difference between them. Let's look at the illustration below. The price increases from A to B before retracing back to C. The time between A and B and between B and C should be the same, and it can be with any number of periods, not just the Kihon Suchi numbers.

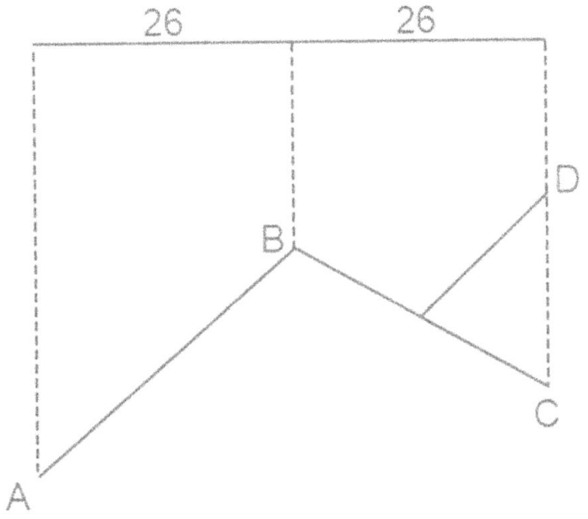

Figure 3-2: Kihon Suchi time cycle

So, when you measure the distance from A to B and find it's 11 bars in between, then it can also be 11 candlesticks from B to C or sometimes from B to D. This is how you analyze the market behavior from a time perspective. In conclusion, Kihon Suchi is the series of numbers (including 9, 17, 26, and other numbers made from them) that provides us a potential distance (calculated by candlesticks) for a reversal point in the market. It's just like a psychological time period that traders can bare to hold their positions. Taito Suchi is where the same numbers appear in the market. It can be one of the Kihon Suchi numbers, but can also be with any other numbers.

This drives us to the third point – the Henka-bi, simply translated as "a day of change". In a financial chart, it is illustrated by a major turning point, either a swing high or a swing low. In the figure above, we have 4 Henka-bi: A, B, C, and D. Notice these Henka-bi points mark the end or start of a cycle. There might be one or two candlesticks difference (a two-bar difference is only allowed for a period of 26 candlesticks or more) between Henka-bi. The idea of using Henka-bi is to pre-define future time milestones so that we can be psychologically ready for the next market reversals.

Now, let's look at a recent chart to see how these numbers show up.

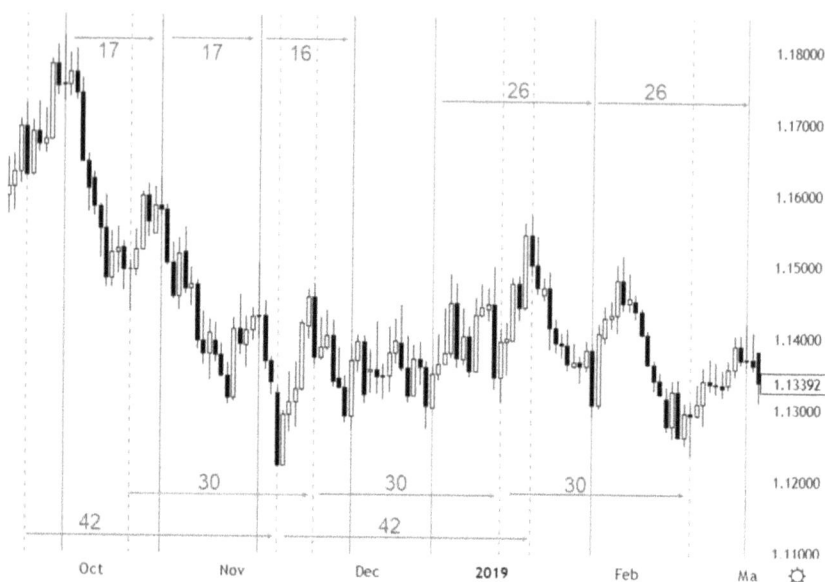

Figure 3-3: EUR/USD time cycle

This is the Daily chart of EUR/USD. If you look at this chart without any indicators, you can clearly see the price actions and trends. Now, with vertical lines plotted at key turning points in the chart, we count the number of candlesticks on each interval and try to find a certain pattern (ideally following the Kihon Suchi rule). As you can see, I've marked the number of candlesticks between different Henka-bi.

On the higher part of the chart, we have 17-bar and 26-bar periods respectively. These periods' lengths are based on the Kihon Suchi numbers. Meanwhile, on the lower part of the chart, by using different starting points, we have the 30-bar (Taito Suchi) and 42-bar (Kihon Suchi) periods. Generally, nearly all major Henka-bi fall in a time cycle. This tells us the power of the time element, and why it's _everything in the market_.

As you can see, the market can move in a Kihon Suchi cycle, which is 17 at the beginning of the downtrend. However, the number of candlesticks within a

46

cycle doesn't necessarily originate from the Kihon-Suchi series, for example, the 30-day cycle. When the market doesn't move with the Kihon Suchi rule, but still with the same number of candlesticks within the cycle, this is called "Taito Suchi", as I mentioned earlier.

To identify these patterns, you'll need to take some time observing a chart, identifying the highs and lows, and counting the candlesticks in between. You can start with the highest or lowest price on a chart, then count the number of candlesticks to the nearest highs or lows going forward or backward, and see if the market resonates with those numbers. To me, it would be even better with the presence of Kihon Suchi numbers when going back and forth with the counting process. If you are using the *tradingview* platform, you can use one powerful tool to make your counting process much quicker and more convenient. Visit http://bit.ly/3GQRIGW to download the tool for free.

Note: you may find other gifts in the download folder. Feel free to download them, too.

Some Taito Suchi variations

Now, let's take one step further with Taito Suchi. Basically, there are some variations in Taito Suchi, and I'm going to show you how they actually appear on a chart. These also play an important part in understanding the time theory, and you may find them quite frequently on financial charts.

Until now, we've discussed the normal Taito Suchi which includes consecutive intervals. Yet, there are also two variations called "***Jugi***" and "***Kakugi***".

1.16000

1.15000

1.14000

1.13000

1.12000

Overlapping
zone

1.10000

45 candlesticks

1.09000

45 candlesticks

1.08000

Figure 3-4: Jugi time cycle

Take a look at this chart. We have two price ranges with 45 candlesticks each, so we have a 45-candlestick time cycle in this example. However, unlike the normal time cycle, in this case, the two price ranges share a small overlapping zone which includes seven candlesticks. When this happens, we call it *Jugi*. When we talk about Jugi, just imagine a small part in common between the two price zones.

Now, take a look at the second type of variation below.

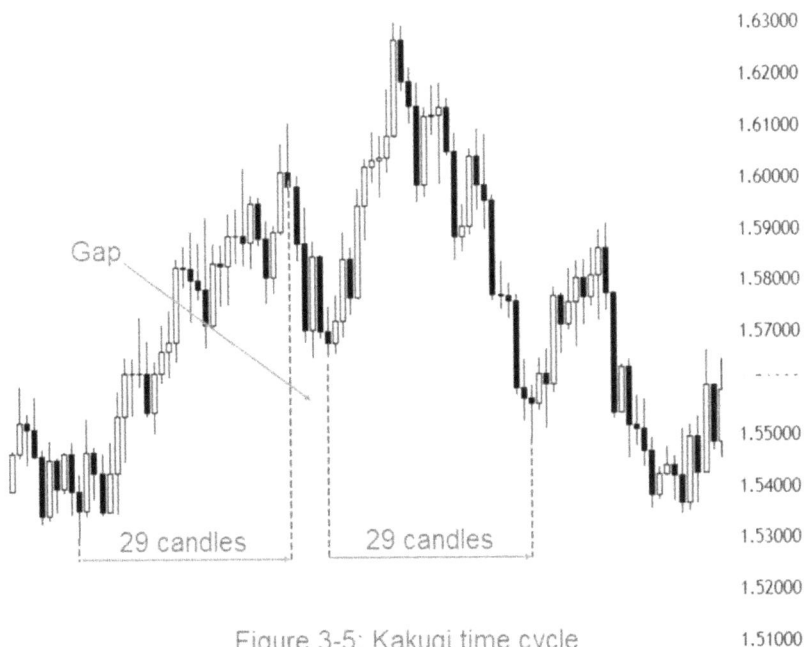

Figure 3-5: Kakugi time cycle

In this example, we have the 27-candlestick time cycle. The market seems to follow the time principle where some major lows and highs appear right at the vertical line of the time cycle. However, there is clearly a small gap between the two price ranges. In this case, we call the pattern **Kakugi**. Notice that when the gap is too wide, it's not called Kakugi. Basically, the gap should be less than half the number of candles in a particular time cycle. In this case, because the cycle includes 27 candlesticks, the gap should be something less than 13. In general, the smaller, the better.

A perfect combination of Tenkan-Sen/Kijun-Sen with the time theory

Now that you've gained a good understanding of the time theory, let's move on further to discover the great relationship between the Tenkan-Sen/Kijun-Sen with this magical theory. I'll explain the meanings of Tenkan-Sen/Kijun-Sen in a close connection with the time theory so that you can fully grasp what these lines are really for, and you will clearly see that they are different from the moving average indicator.

49

Figure 3-6: Time cycle with Tenkan-sen

Here is the Daily chart of USDJPY, and let's focus on the Tenkan-Sen only - the line that shows the half-price level between the highest and the lowest of the past 9 days. Now, let's apply the time theory to Tenkan-Sen. Notice that I've plotted the vertical lines with 9-day intervals and numbered all of them.

Do you find any interesting thing in this example? First, notice how the time of the candlesticks - Tenkan-Sen crossover tends to correspond with the numbered vertical lines. For example, look at the vertical lines between 4 and 7, where the candlesticks were crossing over the Tenkan-Sen up and down every 9 days. It means the cycle of the market between line 4 and line 7 follows the time cycle.

So, why does this happen? Why do these candlesticks cross over the Tenkan-Sen following the 9-day cycle? That's because it's the equilibrium point where the buy and sell powers generally reach a balance, and the price may break towards either direction by following the winner. In other words, it indicates the point where the equilibrium in the market may collapse on the next momentum.

50

Imagine when the price is below Tenkan-Sen and is getting closer to the line. At this stage, it's the bears who are stronger, and the Tenkan-Sen indicates the sell positions have got an advantage for the past 9 days. But as it gets closer to the Tenkan-Sen, it gets closer to equilibrium. When the price finally touches the line, that's when buy and sell powers become equally balanced. So, what can we expect to happen next? If buyers are stronger, the power balance will collapse and the price will break the Tenkan-Sen upwards. On the contrary, if sellers are stronger, the price will be resisted by the Tenkan-Sen and will start to go downwards.

By using the time theory, you can expect where the next equilibrium point will be, but we never know which direction it will move afterward. If we refer to Ichimoku Sanjin's philosophy, we are not here to predict the future of the market but to know the presence of the market. By this, he means to know the time cycle, wave patterns, and potential price targets. All the lines within the Ichimoku Kinko Hyo context are used to expect the time cycle or the rhythm of the market. Using this tool, you will know exactly in what cycle the current price is at.

Now, let's switch to Kijun-Sen. Remember that Kijun-Sen shows the mid-price of the highest and the lowest for the past 26 candlesticks (and 26 is also one of the base numbers). Let's look at the chart below.

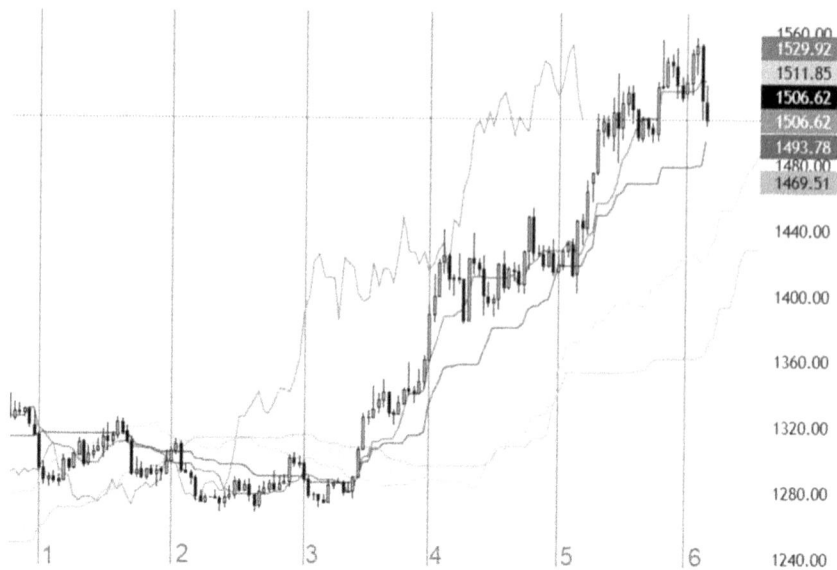

Figure 3-7: Time cycle with Kijun-sen

Here is a Daily chart of Gold. In general, the price has respected the time theory and tends to cross over the Kijun-Sen for every 26-candlestick period. Considering this and the fact that there have been only 4 bars in the current cycle, you can expect the price will reach the next time milestone in 22 trading days. That's when the buy and sell powers become balanced.

From my experience, Ichimoku Kinko Hyo theories work best in the daily time frame or longer, but you can apply them on other time frames such as the 4-hour, 1-hour, or even 5-minute chart because the market is fractal by nature. One thing to remember: on lower time frames (especially 30-mins and below), the market may experience more unexpected price spikes which in turn may affect your analysis negatively.

So, these are some basic ideas on how to use the Tenkan-Sen and Kijun-Sen under the eyes of a time cycle analyst. By looking backward at 9 or 26 candles from where the price touches or crosses these lines, you can get a good idea of whether the market synchronizes with the cycle. If it does, you can expect the market to move with that cycle in the future.

This happens everywhere on any assets or currency pairs because these cycles are considered to be universal. It's just like the psychological cycles that traders can bear to hold on their trades. The real uniqueness of the time theory is to provide the equilibrium price on the market, and how long a cycle is, from that you can know the **presence of the price level** in trading. Ultimately, the time theory works as a base to expect what may happen next in the market, from that, you can create your own trading scenario, just like creating your own business plan for each trade.

So, we've gone over the time cycle, its components, and how to identify them on a financial chart to make the best use of the theory.

The time principle alone can provide valuable insights into the trends, swing lows and highs, and potential trend reversals in the market. Remember it's just the first theory of the three magical ones. Time theory can be much more powerful when combined with wave theory and price theory, which will be introduced next in this chapter. But for now, you may understand why it is so appreciated by the father of the Ichimoku Kinko Hyo.

By practicing more and more with real charts, you can be the master of identifying the presence of the price based on the time cycle and can look at the market from a different angle that other traders may have no idea about.

Wave Theory

We've just explored how the time theory connects nicely with Tenkan-Sen and Kijun-Sen in forecasting the next turning points.

In this section, we'll be talking about different types of wave patterns in a straightforward way. The names of the waves result from the letters they resemble. There are waves that will be seen more often than others. We will present all of them in the section to help you grasp an overview of the wave theory within the Ichimoku context. With some recent chart examples, I hope this will open more ways of recognizing price patterns and identifying high-probability trade setups. Also, I'll talk about how to combine the time and wave theories together.

With that being said, let's get started with some types of waves on the chart under the Ichimoku theory. As for the price movement in the market, there are basically six patterns as shown in the illustration below.

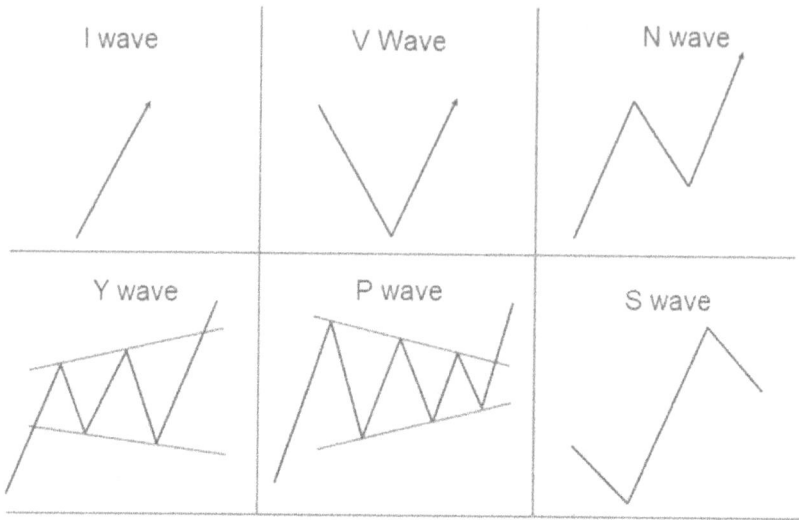

Figure 3-8: Types of waves

- **I wave**

Now, the first pattern on the chart is the I wave. When we think about a trending market, the price will go either up or down. Of course, there are often some retracement efforts or some decreases in the momentum within an overall major trend. However, when you look at the movement of the price, there are only two major trends: bullish and bearish. When there is *no discernable retracement*, we'll call the pattern the I wave - just like the letter I. Basically, the I wave is the simplest wave pattern, either from a low to a high or from a high to a low.

I wave - the simple single wave

- *V Wave:*

This wave occurs in the market when the price reverses after a trending movement, either from ups to downs or from downs to ups.

A "V" wave has two consecutive I waves, either a combination of bullish I wave and bearish I wave, or bearish I wave and bullish I wave. The shape of this wave looks like the letter V (and the inverse of V as well), so it is called a **V wave**.

V Wave - one of the most common patterns

- *N Wave*

When we put an I wave and a V wave together, we'll have an N wave as can be seen to the right of the figure above. In other words, an N wave consists of three consecutive I waves. If you've read my best-selling book "Elliott Wave – Fibonacci High Probability Trading", you'll see the N wave resembles a zigzag pattern in the Elliott Wave context.

N Wave - another common pattern in technical analysis

Note that the patterns in the Figure 3-8 illustrates waves in an uptrend. In case of a downtrend, things will be the opposite.

Also, in the illustration above, we have three less common variations: Y wave, P wave, and S wave. Compared with the other two, the P wave appears more often on a financial chart. It looks like a squeezing flag pattern to whoever familiar with the Elliott Wave theory. On the contrary, the Y and S waves are relatively more difficult to find on a chart from my experience.

P Wave

P Wave - the indication of a sideways market

These three variations often appear as a consolidation chart pattern. Basically, we'll follow the major trend when dealing with a temporary consolidation phase. When the major trend is bullish, we'll trade toward the bullish direction, and vice versa. This is mostly true with the P wave. When you see this pattern on a market, the price will most likely break the consolidation range and resume with the dominant trend.

Sometimes, the Y wave can be a reversal pattern. In that case, we may need the time theory to forecast a high probability reversal zone, which is the Henka Bi as mentioned. Finding a Henka Bi is the aim of every trader in the market. And, with the help of the time theory, it would be much easier.

I hope you'll grasp the basics of the different types of waves in the market. It's quite straightforward and nothing is complicated. The wave theory seems easy to grasp, but the value behind these patterns is timeless and can be applied in many cases to determine entry, stop-loss, and exit prices.

A perfect combination between time theory and wave theory

Now that you've had some basic understanding of the wave theory, let's see how it can be combined with the time theory.

Let's say there's a bullish market in place. You decide to measure how long it took from the beginning to the end of a trend, and find it to be 26 days. If that's the case, then what might happen for the next 26 days in the future could be one of the patterns below.

The first possible pattern would be the I wave, meaning that from its temporary highest, the price might make an opposite movement without any noticeable retracements (the bearish I wave).

The second possibility would be the V wave, meaning that the price may go down initially but find support somewhere along the way. From the end of the retracement, it continues the upward price momentum and finds another high to complete the 26-period time cycle.

The third possible pattern would be an N wave where the price starts with a downward move, then comes a minor retracement before the pullback resumes and forms a lower low to complete the 26-day cycle.

The fourth type of wave would be the S wave, where a minor retracement appears first, then a resume with the prevailing uptrend, and finally another retracement at a Henka-bi. Also, the price can witness a consolidation period in the shape of a P wave or Y wave, which entails watching price actions more thoroughly. In general, the P wave and Y wave are more difficult to recognize in combination with the time theory.

This is basically how you combine time theory and wave theory to determine where the last leg (or the last candlesticks) of a wave may end.

I wave + N wave

V wave + V wave

N wave + V wave

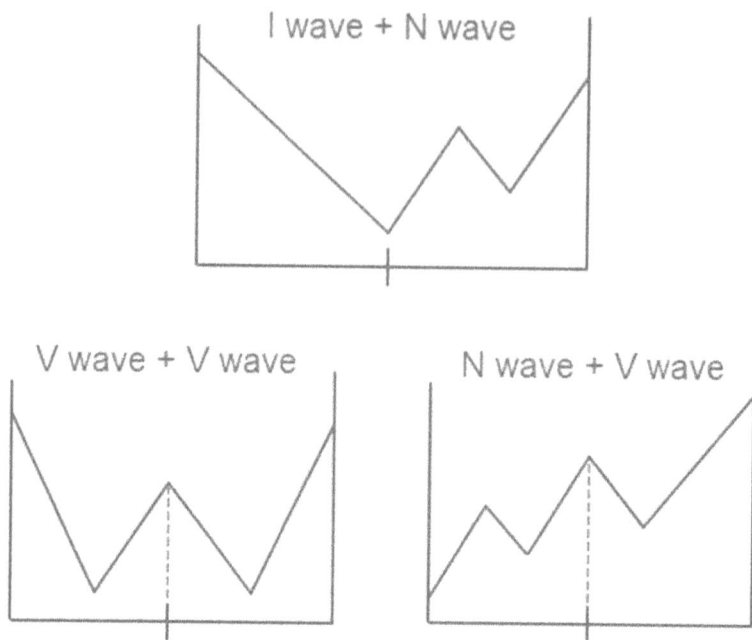

Figure 3-9: Wave combination

Now, remember that the market is full of volatility, and a medium-to-long period (26 bars and above) might witness a lot of ups and downs in the price action. In some hypothetical cases in the figure above, we can see some common combinations of wave patterns in the financial charts. **The first** one would be the I wave – N wave. The price initially keeps going down in an I shape with one of the Kihon Suchi/ Taito Suchi periods (9, 17, 26, or 33). After that, it goes up with the same number of days, but in the shape of an N wave. **The second** combination looks like the W letter, where two V waves are combined. The first V wave starts with a down wave, then it is supported and goes up to about half of the previous movement. In the next cycle, the price goes down again to test the support level and then reverses to revisit the highest price level in the pattern. Classical trade analysts typically call it the *double-bottom* pattern. So, when you calculate the first V and the second V, you might be able to find a certain time cycle. *The last* combination occurs with an N wave and a V wave. The price moves in an N wave shape for the first Taito-Suchi time period, then another move with the same time length in a V wave. In the illustration above, we can see a typical uptrend with higher highs and higher lows.

Again, with the same time cycle, there can be a little difference like 1 or 2 candles. But with a similar number of candlesticks, the market can move with either I, V, N, or some less common types of wave within its cycles, which creates a perfect combination between the wave and time cycle for entry and exit purposes. We'll learn about one strategy based on this combination in the following parts of the book. Now, let's discover the last theory in the list which helps you to identify the profit-taking price level.

Price Observation Theory

The last theory in the list is the *price observation theory*, or *price theory* for short. The single most important purpose of this theory is to provide potential take-profit levels. Using four mathematical formulas, the price theory helps traders to pre-define high-probability trade exit points – the hardest part in financial trading.

The main principle in calculating potential profit targets is to find the *fourth point* of an N wave, simple as that. In other words, with this theory, we'll need to find the first three points in an N wave, and then take the relevant price levels to calculate where the price may extend in the future. We'll first focus on the detailed calculation of each method to get a better understanding of the techniques. As I mentioned earlier, the best thing to understand any trading technique or indicator is by exploring its calculation.

There are four main types of calculations that we'll explore. Let's look at the picture below.

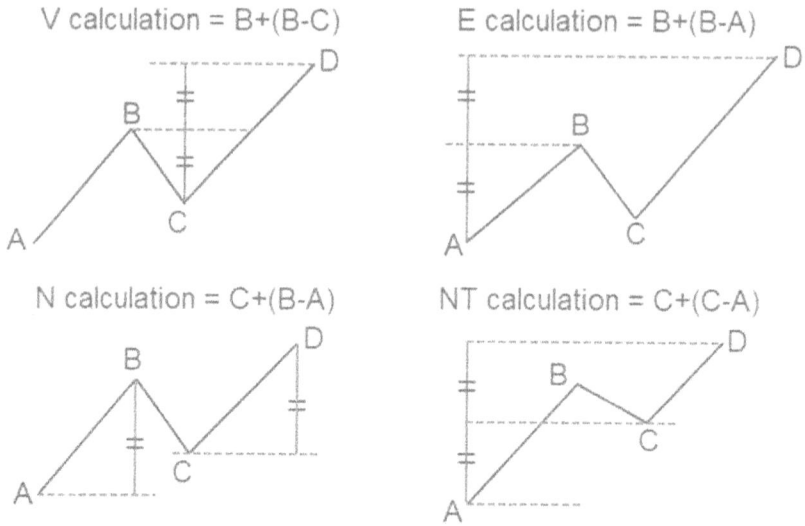

V calculation = B+(B-C)

E calculation = B+(B-A)

N calculation = C+(B-A)

NT calculation = C+(C-A)

Figure 3-10: Price Theory

Let's say the market starts at point A and you are having a buy position slightly above that point. As you observe the market, it goes up to point B, but then came back to point C. Now, we have the first three points of an N wave (A-B-C). The next and most important step is to look for where to take the profit. In that case, you can use one of the four calculations above to identify the potential target. And you'll do it by taking the prices at A, B, and C to calculate out the point D.

The first profit determination method is often called the **V calculation**. The idea is simple. Basically, you'll calculate the distance from B to C, and then add it to the B price. Then, the distance from C to B is equal to that from B to D. This is the V calculation, very simple.

Next on the list, we have the **E calculation**. With this method, you'll take the distance from A to B and add that distance to the price of point B, regardless of how deep the pullback is, to get the price D. In other words, the A-B distance is the same as the B-D distance.

It should be noted that the BC retracement phase couldn't be longer than the initial AB phase. If C is lower than A in this case, BC will not be a retracement phase anymore, but a potential first leg of a reversal.

Now, let's move on to the **N calculation**. With this technique, you'll take the distance from A to B and add that to the C price to get the D point. In this case, the A-B distance will be the same as the C-D distance.

Moving on to the **NT calculation**. Using this method, you'll calculate the distance between C and A and add it to C so that the A-C length and the C-D length will be the same.

Tips: Instead of remembering the formulas, let's look at the comparison between phases (A-B, C-D, A-C, and B-D, or B-C) to identify the potential D point more quickly. For example, you can measure the B-C distance and project that to the end of B to get a possible D point under the V calculation method.

Trading based on the theories

Now that we've gone over three theories in the Ichimoku context, let's combine them to see how you can identify a trade opportunity just based on the theories alone.

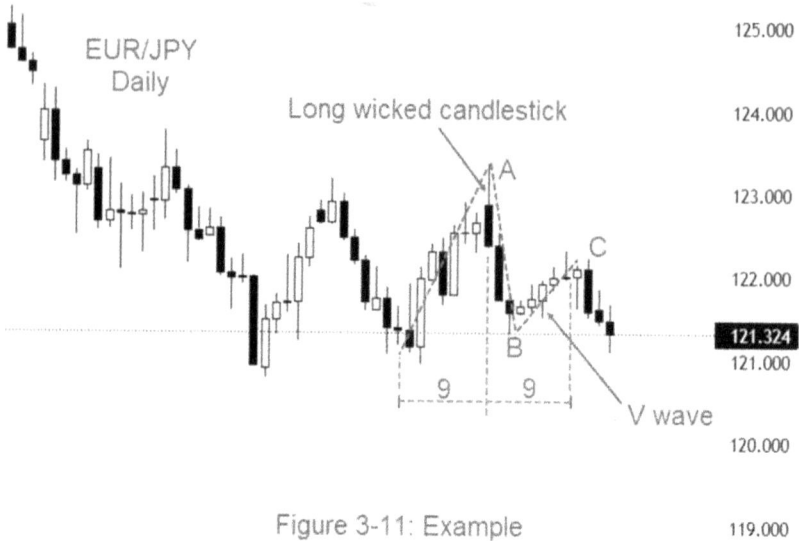

EUR/JPY
Daily

Long wicked candlestick

A

C

B

9   9

V wave

125.000

124.000

123.000

122.000

121.324

121.000

120.000

Figure 3-11: Example

119.000

This is the daily chart of EUR/JPY. After recharging their energies, the bears are ready to resume the trend. You're about to go short, but not quite sure where to place the sell trade. Now, let's employ the theories to find a trade idea in this case.

First, when you look at the chart, you see a V wave with a 9-day interval as indicated. If you go 9 days backward, you can find a swing low which also follows the time principle (9-bar length), thus we now have two consecutive patterns. Notice the candlestick connecting the I wave and the V wave has a long wick pointing upward, meaning that the price action has now favored a downtrend rather than an uptrend.

Until now, you might be more confident to place a sell trade. As you hold the position, the price starts to go down from C. The next and most important task lies in where to take profits. From my experience, taking profits is much more difficult than entering a trade. We are basically greedy, and you may have a dilemma of when to take profits most of the time. If you close your trade too early, the price might extend afterward and cause you regret, which may result in adding more trade arbitrarily. On the contrary, if the closing decision is made too late, your profit will turn into a loss.

Now, the price observation theory can provide potential closing positions based on the prices of the first three points within the N wave. Using the four different ways of calculating the targets, you'll get 4 different targets. After determining these four targets, you'll need to wait for the price reactions at these points to determine your exit price.

This is basically how you can initially calculate the target. I would always recommend traders combine this technique with other tools and indicators to reach a confluence effect in trading where at least two tools release the same trade signal. In this case, if your calculated potential target coincides with a key support or resistance level, it could be a high-probability trade exit point.

Let's look at another example.

Figure 3-12: Example

This is a daily chart of EURGBP. From A, the price went up to B before retracing to C. Let's say you are not having any positions at this point, and things might be favorable for a trend continuation. First, you find the market is on a 10-day cycle as indicated on the chart, so you can imagine that in the next three days, the market might reach a new swing high to complete a cycle. Then, you start to calculate with those 4 calculation methods and mark those levels beforehand so that you can have some ideas of when the price is likely to be reversed, taking price action and other indicators into account. Below is what happened next.

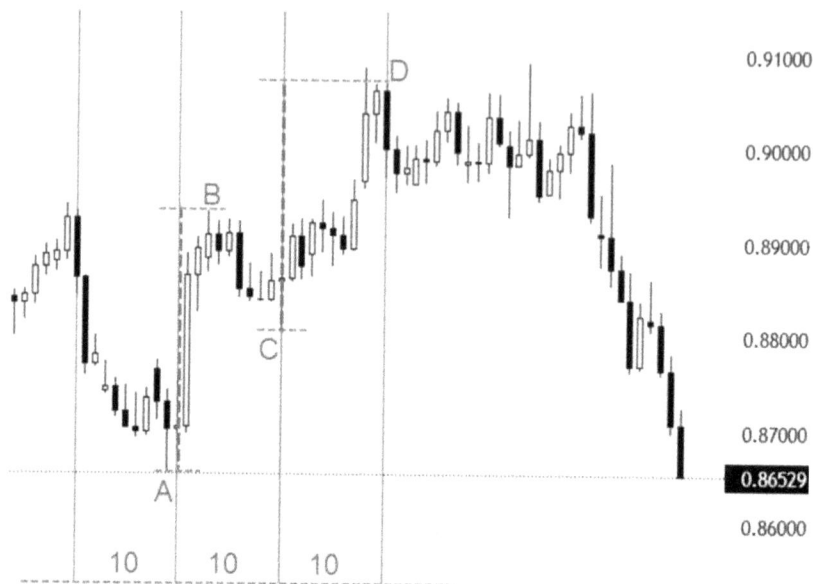

Figure 3-13: Example

As time goes by, the price finally reached the D point which is determined by the N calculation (the A-B length is equal to the C-D length). Notice the price encountered great selling pressure when it first reached this target. This is when you should be ready to close your position. A short consolidation period followed and the price did come back to the NT level once more time before plummeting to the downside. Note that these calculated price levels are not telling exactly which level the price will reach. They serve as targets only, which can be achieved or not. You'll need to read what the market is telling you to deliver the best exit decision.

This brings us to the end of the chapter. This is not a short chapter, but I've tried to convey everything in this chapter in a clear and most concise way possible. I would say the three theories should be applied in combination with other tools and indicators to optimize their use. However, even if they work individually, they can provide a lot of insights into the market trend, price reversal, and profit targets. Again, many trading materials out there tend to overlook these superb aspects in the Ichimoku system. I want to congratulate you on having grasped these great ideas and techniques.

Until now, we've covered many elements from different angles within the Ichimoku toolset. You've now grasped the five lines, their calculations, reflections, and uses. You've also understood different theories which indicate different market insights. Moreover, we've learned how to connect the lines with time theory to get a better picture of the price action and potential market reversals. Although I don't say this is all within the Ichimoku context, I'm confident they are the core of every Ichimoku-based trading system. The next three chapters will focus on the most important part of the book – trading strategies based on the power of Ichimoku theories and magical lines. I believe you've been expecting this for long, so without any further ado, let's jump into Chapter 4.

CHAPTER 4: THE VOICE OF THE CROSS

In Chapter 2, we discussed the gold cross and death cross in a trending market. We talked about signals of a reliable cross as well as discovering the checklist of a vulnerable cross between the two lines. You've now gained some fundamental yet important knowledge of identifying trade opportunities with gold crosses and death crosses.

In this chapter, we'll discuss the first strategy in trading with Ichimoku based on Kinko Hyo crossovers. You'll explore how to identify trade opportunities in great detail right from the beginning of the trend. At the end of the chapter, you'll have a clear and reliable checklist of what to expect and monitor to make the best use of price movements as well as how to identify the entry, stop-loss, and profit targets.

To start with, let's first explore the second type of market movement – the sideways movement. More specifically, we'll talk more about how a typical cross looks like in a consolidation range. As you may already know, this is the market condition in which I rarely place a trade, so you might wonder why I choose this "risky" market to start with. A simple answer is that it can help us to find the best market timing and let the most possible profits run.

Crosses in a range-bound market

This is the second part of " Kinko Hyo Gold Cross and Death Cross", but I present it in this chapter because it is directly linked to the entry of the crossover technique.

Many of the trend-related technical indicators are effective when there is a trend, but Ichimoku Kinko Hyo becomes a valuable technical indicator during a consolidation period as well. In the case of a sideways market, both Tenkan-Sen and Kijun-Sen show the center price of the consolidation range.

When the market is in a range, Ichimoku lines tend to get closer and some of them may remain flat. We can easily see horizontal lines which indicate the exact central price level of the range market. In the chart below, there is a clear sideways range in the market. Take a closer look at the movements of the five lines.

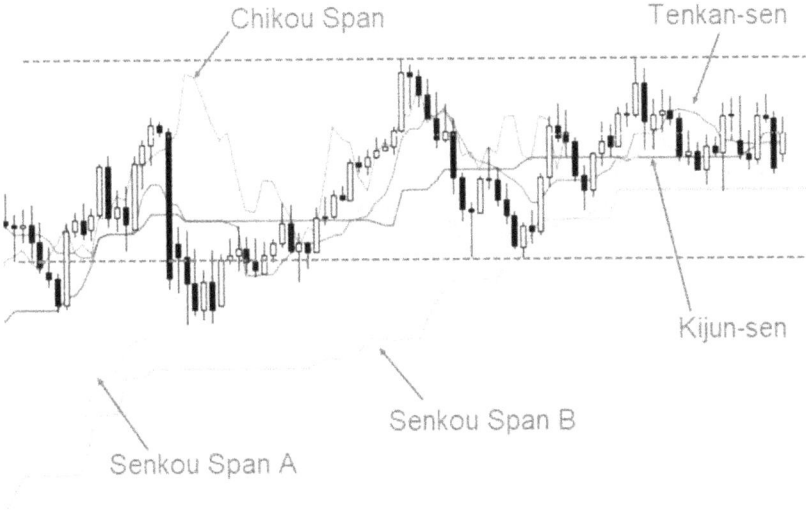

Figure 4-1: Ichimoku lines in a range-bound market

You can see that each line becomes flat at some point in the range, except for Chikou Span. Due to its nature, the Chikou Span can hardly become flat in any chart. If the highest and lowest prices remain the same for a long time within a period of 26 candlesticks or less, both the Kijun-Sen and Tenkan-Sen will remain at the same price level, and sometimes overlap for a period of time.

Still, in the example above, Senko span 2 is staying slightly below the Kijun-Sen. Basically, the Kijun-Sen indicates the center of the current 26 candles but the Senko span 2 takes the center of the 52 candles and forward the mid-price level 26 candles later, so there is a time lag between Kijun-Sen and Senko Span 2.

69

A sideways range is characterized by lines crossing and overlapping. Put differently, Tenkan-Sen and Kijun-Sen tend to be close to each other instead of moving far away as in a trending market. Now, let's discover different consolidation ranges in the market.

Range Type 1: High volatility range

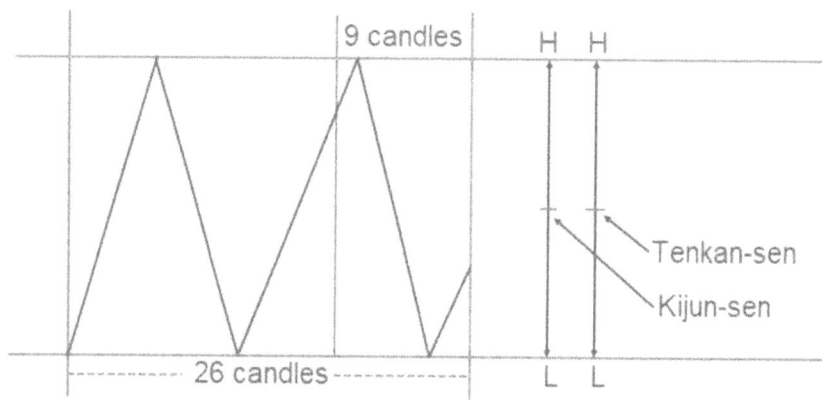

Figure 4-2: High volatility range

In the illustration above, the cycle is repeated within the same high and the same low, which looks like the "W" or "M" shape. Notice the price moves between the two bands with a similar momentum, either in an uptrend or a downtrend. This can be a nightmare for trend-following traders because their stop-loss can easily be hit. Also, notice the 26-period high is equal to the 9-period high, and the 26-period low equals the 9-period low. This results in the same price level between Kijun-Sen and Tenkan-Sen. This is a typical range pattern that we see a lot in financial charts.

Range Type 2: P-wave range

The next type of consolidation would be when the market loses its volatility gradually. Take a look at the figure below.

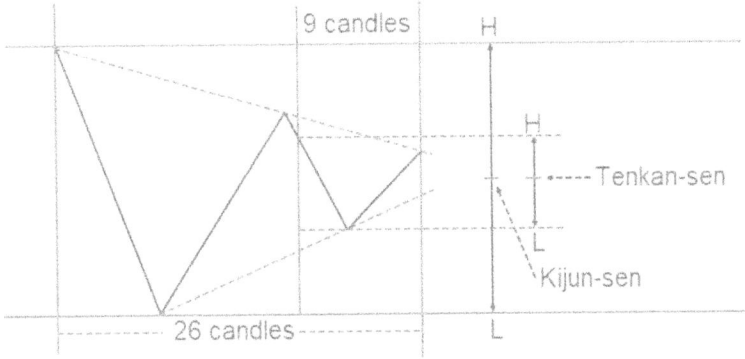

Figure 4-3: P-wave range

A range that gradually shrinks down is usually referred to as the "P wave" in the Ichimoku Kinko Hyo context. The movement of the last 9 candlesticks of the P wave comes within the center of the price movements of the last 26 candles. In other words, the high and low are determined at the beginning of the 26-candlestick period. As a result, the Tenkan-Sen and Kijun-Sen overlap.

Range Type 3: Y-wave range

The third type of consolidation is opposite to the second type. It's when the market increases its volatility as it progresses. Let's look at the figure below.

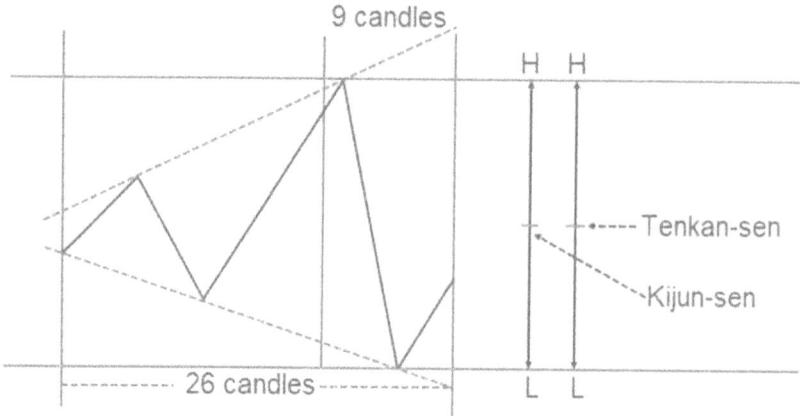

Figure 4-4: Y-wave range

A range with increasing volatility is usually referred to as a "Y wave" in the Ichimoku Kinko Hyo context. When the widest part between the high and the low is marked within the last 9 candles, the Tenkan-Sen and The Kijun-Sen will overlap. The Y wave and its deformations are quite commonly seen. For example, the uprising price suddenly drops to the point where the 26-candle low is renewed. And the dropped price then spikes up to the point where it renews the 26-candle high. Eventually, the highest and lowest prices for the past 9 candles will be the same as those for the past 26 candles.

Range Type 4: Volatile Y-wave range

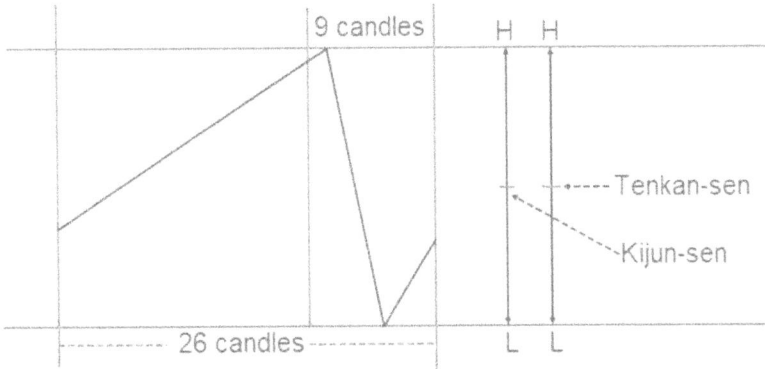

Figure 4-5: Volatile Y-wave range

This is also a type of Y wave, but the price action is so volatile in the last 9 candles. This type of price action is generally not very popular in the market. Its movement is quite unexpected, which is often caused by hot news. Trading in this market can put traders in a lot of danger.

Until now, we've discussed the different types of consolidation ranges and some characteristics of each range. While some traders are interested in trading the ups and downs within a range, this is generally not a favorable condition to maximize profits. After a range ends, a trend will come. Therefore, the most important message of a (long) consolidation period is to tell us that *a trend might come next*. This drives us to the next concept in this chapter – the range breakout.

Range breakout – the target

Basically, I'm a trend follower. The only case when I favor retracement trading within the Ichimoku context will be disclosed in the next chapter when I share with you the art of multiple timeframe analysis.

To follow the trend, we'll need to find a way to get out of the range with a quite reliable direction, just like when the price tries to get out of the storm to find stability as I mentioned earlier. Let's take a look at the chart below.

73

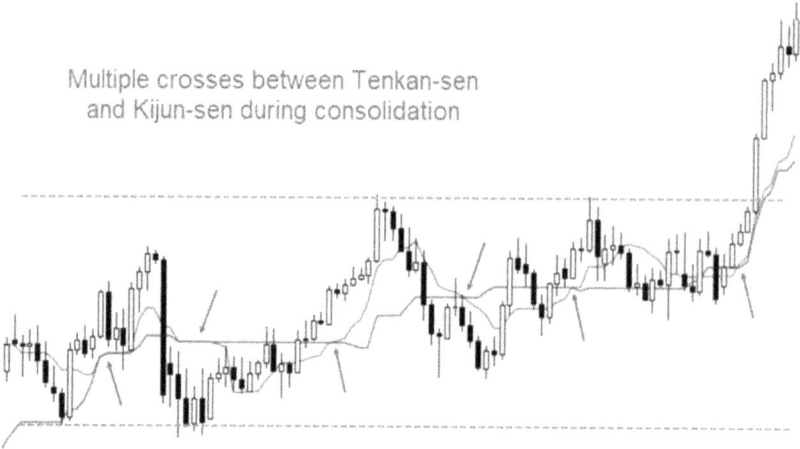

Multiple crosses between Tenkan-sen
and Kijun-sen during consolidation

Figure 4-6: Tenkan-sen & Kijun-sen in a range-bound market

In this example, you can see that the market enters into a consolidation period. The Kijun-Sen indicates the center of the range, and Kijun-Sen and Tenkan-Sen repeatedly cross. These crosses are another reflection that the market is non-trending. As mentioned, we aim to identify a reliable breakout.

A range breakout happens when the price clearly breaks the highest of the range upwards or the lowest of the range downwards and initiates a trend. In general, the longer the consolidation lasts, the more probable a breakout may come. Range breakout happens when the charged energy during the consolidation bursts toward either direction.

In general, the range breakout strategy gives a slow signal because it happens when the highest price or the lowest price is clearly renewed. As stated earlier, the Kijun-Sen and Tenkan-Sen cross happens many times during the range, and most of them become fake crosses that fail to release a trade signal. However, "the last cross before the range ends" and "the first cross after range breakout" would be great signals to take into account. I mentioned earlier that the Hanne lines of Ichimoku Kinko Hyo can tell you the center of a range, and we'll use this characteristic to read what the market wants to tell.

Let's say the price goes down 30 pips from Kijun-Sen in the past, then it's likely to go up 30 pips from Kijun-Sen next time. If the price goes up 40 pips from the Kijun-Sen, then the next time, it's likely to go down 40 pips below the Kijun-Sen. These repeated ups and downs from the Han-ne line show when the market is in a range. This means if the price **does not go up or down from the Han-ne line** anymore, it's the signal that the range might come to an end.

Take a closer look at the chart below. First, you can see that there are many crosses between Tenkan-Sen and Kijun-Sen during the range. Normally, the Kijun-Sen becomes almost flat and the Tenkan-Sen crosses the Kijun-Sen up and down.

Figure 4-7: Tenkan-sen & Kijun-sen in a range-bound market

However, look at the cross circled at the end of the consolidation period. This is completely different from previous crosses. The Tenkan-Sen goes up strongly after the gold cross, and the Kijun-Sen starts to go up later with a decent angle. This Kinko Hyo gold cross is the significant one that implies a possible range breakout.

With these analyses, below is how to read the price action within a consolidation period and prepare for the next breakout move.

- Look for the crosses between the Kijun-Sen and Tenkan-Sen within a range. Normally the Kijun-Sen becomes almost flat while the Tenkan-Sen repeatedly crosses Kijun-Sen from below or above.
- If Tenkan-Sen tends to move toward Kijun-Sen in a short time, that's a sign of continuous range.
- Breakout happens when the Tenkan-Sen starts to increase the gap from the Kijun-Sen. Moreover, when the Kijun-Sen also starts to go up or down, this is also a sign of a potential breakout.

Note that a new trend may start when Tenkan-Sen and Kijun-Sen have a wider gap between them after the cross. When it becomes a steady uptrend, the gap will gradually get wider while both lines are moving up. In contrast, when it's a stable bear trend, the gap between the lines will be wider as the price keeps moving down. It's important to look at the price direction itself as well as the gap between the two Han-ne lines.

How to trade with Kinko Hyo crosses

It is very important to understand what it really means when Tenkan-Sen and Kijun-Sen cross. If you just buy at the gold cross or sell at the death cross just like it says on many websites, that's how kids would trade. If you want to be a master of Ichimoku Kinko Hyo, you need to analyze and understand when and how the gold cross and death cross of Kinko Hyo happen, then you'll know which cross signals you should take a trade.

Let's now go into details of trading the gold cross and death cross within the Ichimoku Kinko Hyo context.

+ Gold Cross

- Observation:

- Start with a consolidation period. The consolidation should occur around a not-quite-big Kumo (ideally a thin Kumo), which is a favorable condition for a range breakout. Carefully observe the crosses between the Kijun-Sen and Tenkan-Sen within a range. Normally, Kijun-Sen becomes almost flat while Tenkan-Sen repeatedly crosses Kijun-Sen from below or above. If the Tenkan-Sen starts moving toward the Kijun-Sen in a short time, that's a sign of continuous range.

-   A breakout might come next if the Tenkan-Sen doesn't return to the Kijun-Sen after the gold cross, and the two lines become (clearly) steeper after the last crossover within the range.

-   Wait for both the gold cross and the range breakout to happen. Keep in mind that a valid range breakout under this method must occur *above the Kumo* (ideally a thin Kumo).

- Determining the entry price and monitoring trades

    Enter the trade at the breakout point. Stop-loss can be placed below the lower boundary of the range, the mid-price of the range, or below the Kumo, depending on each market condition. The take-profit price is determined via the price observation theory or when there are consecutive indecision candlesticks.

- Monitoring the trade to ensure a high probability crossover trade setup:

-   After the cross, the price and Tenkan-Sen go up and increase the distance from the Kijun-Sen. Even if the price comes close to Kijun-Sen temporarily, it should move away and goes up quickly.
-   The Kijun-Sen starts to go up after the bullish Tenkan-Sen is confirmed.
-   The Tenkan-Sen and Kijun-Sen both go up with a certain interval in between.

+ Death Cross

- Observation:

- Start with a consolidation period. The consolidation should occur around a not-quite-big Kumo (ideally a thin Kumo), which is a favorable condition for a range breakout. Carefully observe the crosses between the Kijun-Sen and Tenkan-Sen within a range. Normally, Kijun-Sen becomes almost flat while Tenkan-Sen repeatedly crosses Kijun-Sen from below or above. If the Tenkan-Sen starts moving toward the Kijun-Sen in a short time, that's a sign of continuous range.

- A breakout might come next if the Tenkan-Sen doesn't return to the Kijun-Sen after the death cross, and the two lines become (clearly) steeper after the last crossover within the range.

- Wait for both the death cross and the range breakout to happen. Keep in mind that a valid range breakout under this method must occur *below the Kumo* (ideally a thin Kumo).

- Determining the entry price and monitoring trades

  Enter the trade at the breakout point. Stop-loss can be placed above the higher boundary of the range, the middle price of the range, or above the Kumo, depending on each market condition. The take-profit price is determined via the price observation theory or when there are consecutive indecision candlesticks.

- Monitoring the trade to ensure a high probability crossover trade setup:

- After the cross, the price and Tenkan-Sen go down and increase the distance from the Kijun-Sen. Even if the price comes close to Kijun-Sen temporarily, it should move away and goes down quickly.
- The Kijun-Sen starts to go down after the bearish Tenkan-Sen is confirmed.

- The Tenkan-Sen and Kijun-Sen both go down with a certain interval in between.

Note: The point here is **whether the Tenkan-Sen moves around the Kijun-Sen or moves away from the Kijun-Sen after the crossover.**

+ *Beware of the fake signals:*

- The Kijun-Sen is flat or almost flat.
- Initially, the price and Tenkan-Sen temporarily move away from the Kijun-Sen, but it quickly returns to the Kijun-Sen and crosses again.

Trade examples

Any strategy won't become clearer and meaningful until they are backed up with real trade examples. Now, let's take a look at some trade examples that will be specifically explained so that you'll get the backbone of the strategy.

Trade example 1: Trading EUR/USD gold cross

Take a look at the chart below.

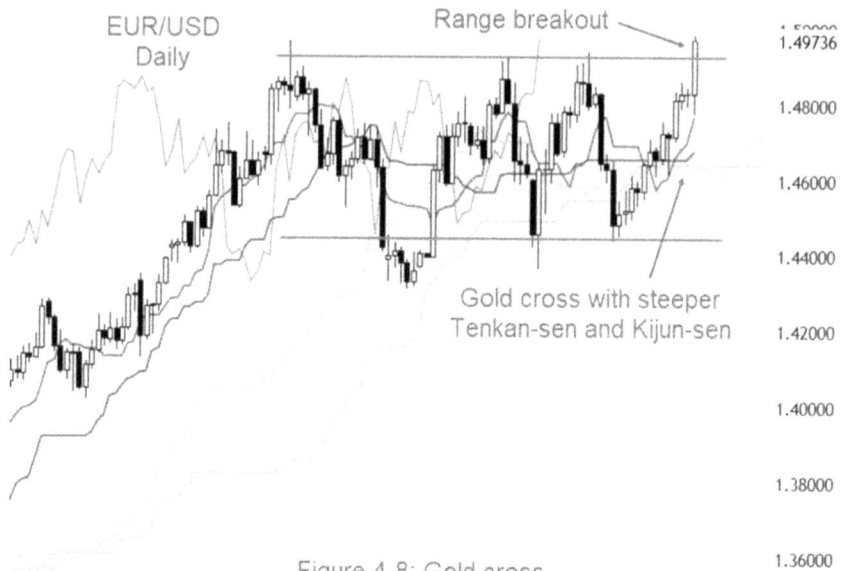

Figure 4-8: Gold cross

In this EUR/USD chart, the market had been in a nice bullish trend before it entered a consolidation period. Notice how the price was held by the Tenkan-Sen during most of its prior bullish movement, indicating that the uptrend was strong. After that, the market was kept in a range marked by two horizontal lines on the chart. This range happened right at the Kumo which was becoming thinner than it was during the prior bullish trend. Moreover, we can see the Tenkan-Sen crossed the Kijun-Sen back and forth— a typical indication of a non-trend market. We should remain on the sidelines during this stage and wait for a range breakout.

After some ups and downs movement, the price successfully closed above the higher border of the range, and both Kijun-Sen and Tenkan-Sen broke above the thin Kumo with a much steeper curve. Moreover, if we look back at 26 periods, the Chikou line also crossed above candlesticks, indicating the bulls had gained some advantages for the last 26 periods. This was an ideal condition for a long entry at the close of the breakout candlestick.

Now, unlike other strategies, the stop-loss shouldn't be something fixated on within the Ichimoku context. To determine a stop price in this case, we should first notice that the Kumo is extremely thin in this case, hence a stop-loss below the Kumo or below the lower border of the range would be acceptable. A conservative trader may prefer a stop below the consolidation zone, which is completely understandable. It depends on your risk tolerance to decide which price level you would choose. Now, let's extend the price action a little more to see how the price reacted with the Tenkan-Sen and Kijun-Sen as well as the price action.

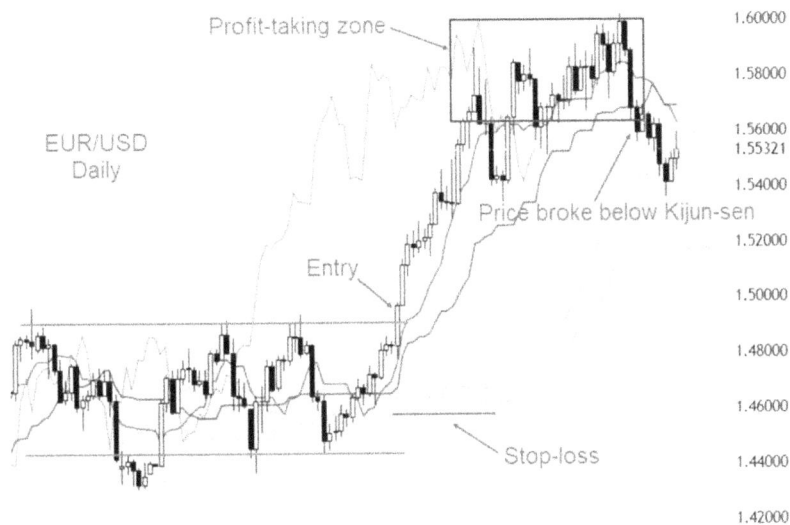

Figure 4-9: Take profit

As you can see, the new bull trend turned out to be a strong trend where the price was held by the Tenkan-Sen for a long period. Also, notice that the distance between the two Han-ne lines increased as the trend progressed. At one point during the progress, the price broke the Tenkan-Sen but failed to reach the Kijun-Sen. At this point, we have the first three points of an N wave, and some traders might have thought of calculating the fourth point of the N wave. However, notice consecutive indecision candlesticks afterward which tell us that the bulls really had difficulties in riding the trend, and the interval between the two Han-ne lines became narrowed as well. This is when we should be prepared for closing the position. The weakness of the trend became clearer when the Kijun-Sen level was broken by the price for the first time after the gold cross. This is when we should consider exiting our position.

81

It should be noted that the price breaking Kijun-Sen doesn't mean that the trend has changed. In this case, I won't say that the bullish trend has reversed. However, if we've ridden the trend a long way with a decent risk-reward ratio, this could be an acceptable profit-taking option.

Trade example 2: Trading USD/JPY death cross

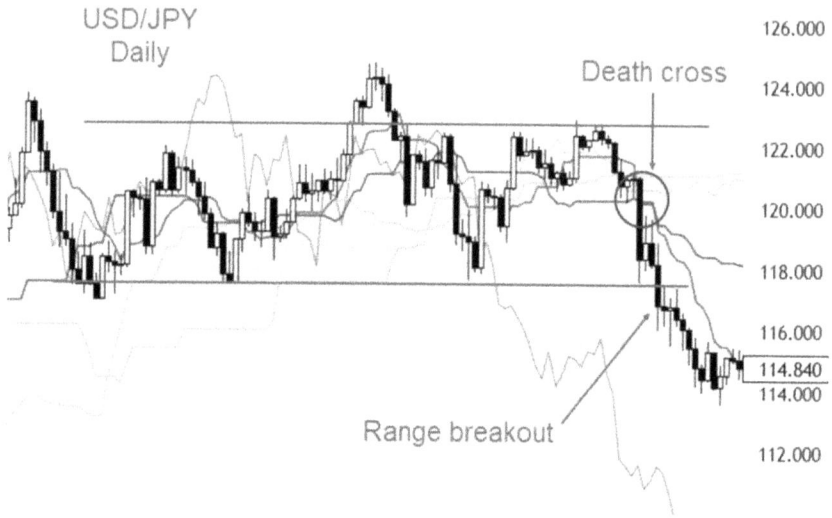

Figure 4-10: Death cross

This is the USD/JPY sideways range on the daily chart. At first glance, this might seem to be a big range. However, taking a closer look at the chart, we can see Kijun-Sen remained flat most of the time, and Tenkan-Sen crossed Kijun-Sen back and forth without signaling a clear direction. These are typical characteristics of a sideways range. Now, one of the most important signals of a potential range breakout is *the Kumo shrank over time*. In most cases, this is when I'll watch closely at the price action and get ready for a breakout trade. In this example, notice how the death cross corresponded with a range breakout, and this breakout fell below the Kumo as well. Furthermore, the Chikou line crossed below the candlesticks, which serves as another supportive trade signal. All these points allow us to place a short entry at the close of the breakout

82

candlestick. The stop-loss could be placed above the Kumo, considering the cloud has become very thin at this point. This stop-loss is safe enough when it's on the other side of the cloud while providing a potentially good risk-reward ratio (not very far from the entry price).

Now, let's employ the price theory to catch the target of the trade.

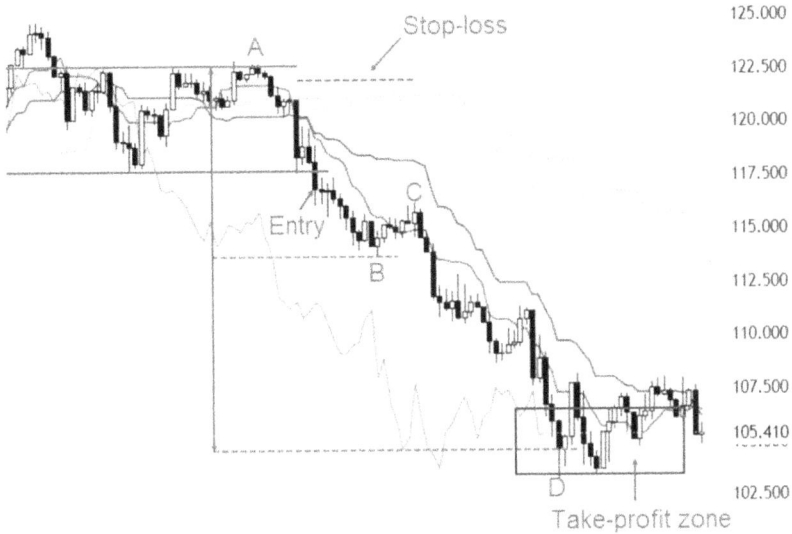

Figure 4-11: Take profit

Now, notice after the death cross, Tenkan-Sen and Kijun-Sen widened the interval between them. This is a positive signal for a continuous downtrend. Soon afterward, the price made a retracement, and we have three points of an N wave. Using the E calculation, we can easily determine the D target, which is near the bottom of the bearish trend as can be seen on the chart. We can achieve a 3-R profit in this case just by combining the death cross, Kumo shape, range breakout, and price theory.

So, we've now covered the first strategy in this book. I hope you've fully understood and enjoyed the process so far. We've learned about the consolidation period in trading, the role of stalking in this tedious market, and how to catch the best entry and stop-loss prices by analyzing a number of factors on the chart. Moreover, we've learned one crucial point that no websites or books have talked about: the connection between the consolidation phase and the trending phase. This makes this strategy unique and timeless.

At this point, you might understand why *"buy on a gold cross"* and *"sell on a death cross"* are only for kids. Trading is all about optimizing factors to put the odds in our favor.

In the next chapter, we'll learn a more advanced strategy and the art of multiple-timeframe trading.

CHAPTER 5: KIJUN-SEN & THE ART OF RETRACEMENT

In this chapter, we'll talk mostly about Kijun-Sen and how it plays an important part in determining entry and take-profit levels. This is quite an advanced strategy where you'll need to analyze market conditions and find trade opportunities based on the movement of the Kijun-Sen before switching to a lower timeframe to optimize entry and exit points. As the chapter title suggests, this is a type of retracement strategy, meaning that you might not be able to let profit run as in the first strategy. However, it's worth exploring and can provide a trading edge to those who truly understand how it works.

This strategy might be strange to a lot of traders, but once you've understood how it operates, you will be amazed at how it performs.

We'll guide you through each concept of the strategy, the momentum behind it, and what to expect in each situation. Most importantly, we'll guide you step-by-step in identifying entry and exit points.

Now, if you're ready, let's get started.

Trade analysis

We've all known that the Kijun-Sen is one of the Han-ne lines within the Ichimoku toolset. Kijun-Sen reflects the equilibrium price (or market price) of an asset for a 26-candlestick period. It's where buyers and sellers reach a consensus, or when supply and demand are balanced. It's the market price that tends to pull the price back after a long interval period.

The idea of trading the Kijun-Sen retracement setup roots from a common observation that Goichi Hosoda mentioned in his original Ichimoku book (this is what most of the books or websites out there don't focus on). As I mentioned in earlier chapters, the price tends to revisit Han-ne lines after a certain period of moving with the trend. The Kijun-Sen reflects the mid-term price movement, hence this is where the price tends to retrace over the mid-term (note that 26 is a Kihon Suchi number). Take a look at the example below.

Figure 5-1: Kjiun-sen and candlesticks

This is the AUD/USD chart example. Note how the price tends to find the Tenkan-Sen for every 26-candlestick period. This indicates the power of the equilibrium price in the market. It works as a magnet to pull the price when the candlestick - Kijun-Sen interval gets prolonged and far away from each other. The Kijun-Sen reflects the rule of supply and demand, which not only prevails in financial trading but also in economics in general: *Higher prices boost supply and cause demand to drop, and lower prices increase demand while limiting supply.*

Note: The example above is an ideal one for explaining the time cycle in connection with Kijun-Sen – price relationship. It should be noted that not all crosses between them happen every 26 periods. It just tends to do so. The average period number for a cross between them is 26 – a Kihon Suchi number.

When the price "forgets" to find the equilibrium price for more than 26 periods, this is when we should pay more attention to the price action, and look for *reliable* market signals to better assess whether the pullback might happen next.

86

Note that not every delayed pullback for more than 26 periods will lead to a successful retracement to the Kijun-sen line. The market goes up and down all the time, and without these filters below, we won't be able to look for a real retracement trade opportunity in the market.

Trade execution

The analyses above can open some ideas of trading against the trend while basing on some timeless principles in trading considering the correlation between the bulls and the bears. Below are some necessary steps in trading Kijun-Sen retracement setups:

1. Determining the last Kijun-Sen break above or below the candlestick; find a prolonged period where the Kijun-Sen hasn't crossed the candlesticks for more than 26 periods;

2. If Kijun-Sen turns horizontal, switch to a lower timeframe, and wait for the price to establish a clearer trend (either a Kumo break or a cross over both Kumo and a key level) to place an entry;

3. Draw the forecast line to assess whether the current price action is above the line (in an overall downtrend) or below the line (in an overall uptrend). If yes, we might be correct with our trade;

4. The take-profit price would be the Kijun-Sen in the higher timeframe. The stop-loss would be just below the last swing low or Kumo (in case of an uptrend retracement) or above the last swing high or Kumo (in case of a downtrend retracement) in the lower timeframe;

Still be difficult to get my ideas. Don't worry, below are some real trade examples with specific analyses to help you get the picture.

Trade examples

Let's take a look at the first example.

USD/CAD
Daily

Kijun-sen turned flat

Senkou Span A and B
were flat

35 candlesticks

Figure 5-2: Trade example 1

This is the USD/CAD daily chart. Note that the current Kumo and Kijun-Sen were flat, and the price was below Tenkan-Sen, meaning that the trend was still bearish.

Now, if you calculate the number of candlesticks dating from the nearest Kijun-Sen – candlestick crossover, the market had been below the Kijun-Sen for the last 35 periods. Remember that the average time for the market to retrace to Kijun-Sen is 26 periods, and 35 is overextended in this case. This means we expect the market to trace back to Kijun-Sen. However, just because Kijun-Sen was flat and had been above the price for more than 26 bars doesn't mean we can blindly take a buy trade. The market could break support and continuously go down. This is why we need to switch to a lower timeframe as in the figure below.

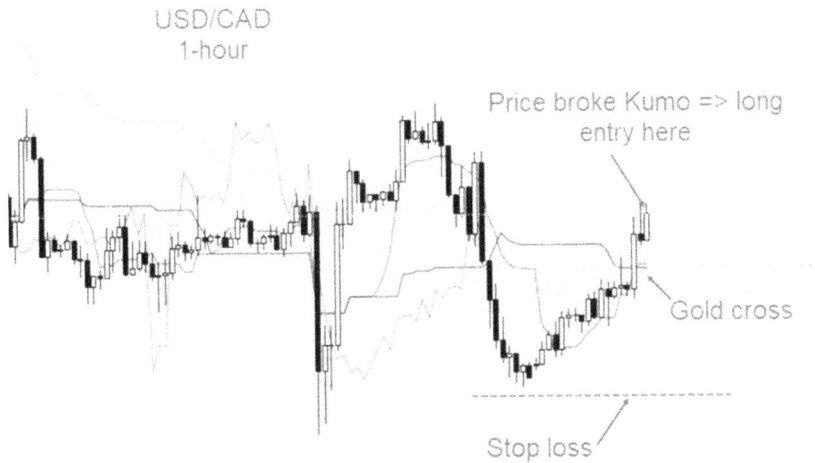

Figure 5-3: 1-hour time frame

In this chart, we've switched to a lower time frame – the one-hour chart. In this timeframe, we'll wait for a clearer and more reliable uptrend, or wait for the price to break the Kumo to enter a buy position. A break above the Kumo provides a higher probability of a retracement. This is important because as I mentioned earlier, not every delayed crossover between the Kijun-Sen and the price would lead to a retracement eventually. In this example, notice the break above Kumo occurred soon after the gold cross which further favored an upward move. We can enter a buy position at the close of the breakout candlestick.

The stop-loss would be placed below the last swing low in this example because this is a bullish order.

You can switch back to the longer timeframe at any time to verify if the retracement phase is flowing smoothly or not. Below was how things turned out after a few more daily candlesticks. As you can see in the figure below, the forecast line was respected.

Figure 5-4: Verify the retracement with the forecast line

If the price didn't break the forecast line downwards, we can be more confident in a successful upward retracement. In this example, the forecast line once again favored a retracement to the Kijun-Sen.

The profit-taking price would be when the price touched the Kijun-Sen on the longer timeframe because we're assuming that the price will retrace back to this Ichimoku line. Look at the figure below.

Figure 5-5: Take-profit price

Notice the profit-taking level on the chart indicates the crossover between the price and the Kijun-Sen on the daily chart. Still, I use the 1-hour chart to help you get the whole picture of what happened during the retracement. As you can see, this is the retracement phase, and the momentum was not as strong as in the trending phase. It did take quite a bit of time to reach the target, but it's worth the wait.

This is the Kijun-Sen and retracement strategy that I want to introduce. I hope you've gotten the core of the strategy.

Noted that a merely flat Kijun-Sen won't be enough for a pullback trade. Take a look at the example below.

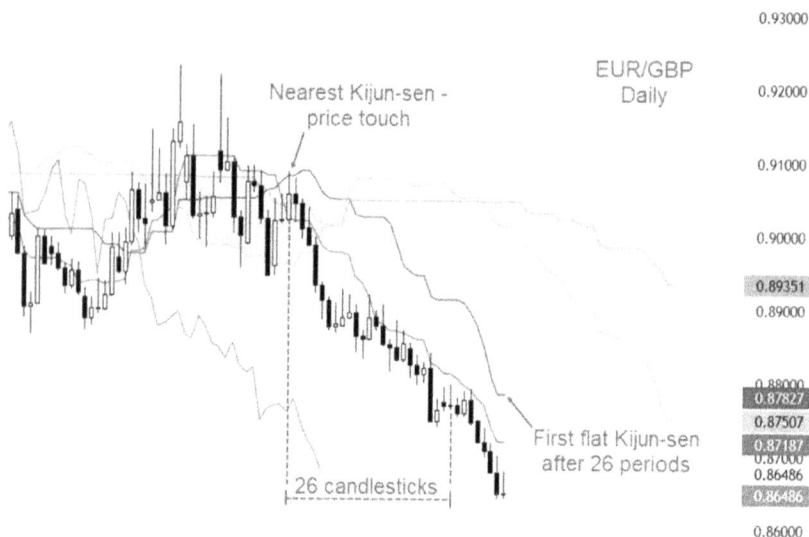

Figure 5-6: Trade example 2

In this chart, I've marked the nearest touch between the price and Kijun-Sen. From this point, the market had been gone all the way down below the Kijun-Sen for quite a long time. Notice that after 26 bars, the market was still far away from the Kijun-Sen. It wasn't until the 8 bars after that the Kijun-Sen became horizontal. In this case, we can move to a shorter timeframe to verify the price action.

EUR/GBP
1-hour

Strong downtrend

Price broke support level

Figure 5-7: Trade example 2 - 1-hour time frame

On the 1-hour timeframe, the price was still below the Kumo, Tenkan-Sen, and Kijun-Sen, and no uptrend signal was present at that time. Moreover, the downward bias is clearer considering the price just broke the latest support level. All these points strengthened the idea that a pullback trade would not be feasible in this example. In this case, what we could do is wait for the next horizontal Kijun-Sen on the longer timeframe, and analyze the relevant price action.

Let's see what happened in a few next candlesticks.

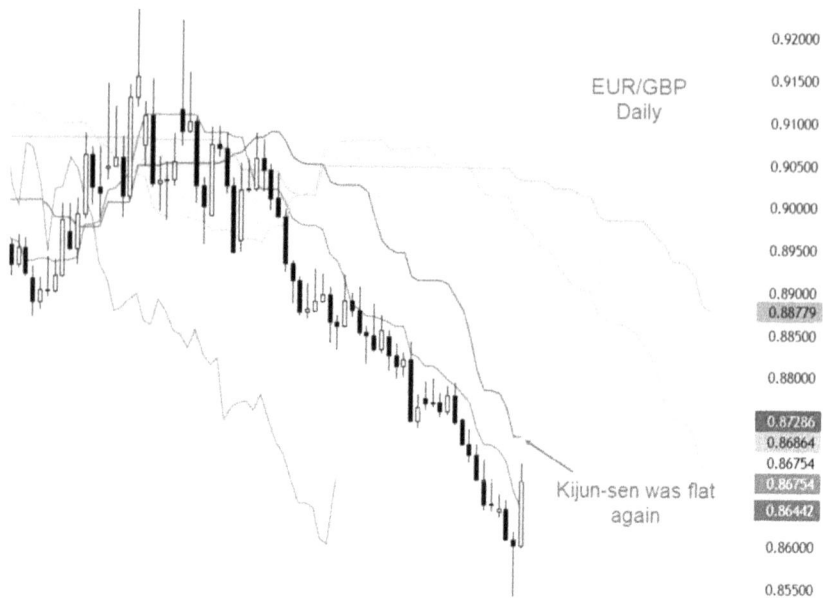

Figure 5-8: Trade example 2 - daily timeframe

The Kijun-Sen went flat again, but this time, things were better than the previous one. Notice two consecutive candlesticks that signaled a possible uptrend: doji and engulfing patterns. Now, let's see what happened in the 1-hour chart.

0.87200

EUR/GBP
1-hour

0.87000

0.86800

0.86600

0.86400

0.86134

0.86134
0.86083
0.85985
0.85963
0.85888

0.85600

0.85400

Figure 5-9: Trade example 2 - favorable condition to take a trade

In the 1-hour chart, the market managed to break above the Kumo, which signaled that the trend might be upward over the short-term. Prior to this break, the Tenkan-Sen crossed above the Kijun-Sen (the gold cross), which is another supportive signal for a potential buy trade. Considering the favorable conditions in both longer and shorter timeframes, we should be more confident in entering a buy entry at the close of the breakout candlesticks. The market condition is quite supportive in this example. If, however, the price is still below the Kumo initially and doesn't signal any trade idea at this point, we just wait until a clearer signal is present. In the figure below, the price easily reached the profit target defined in the longer time frame (when the price successfully revisited the Kijun-Sen).

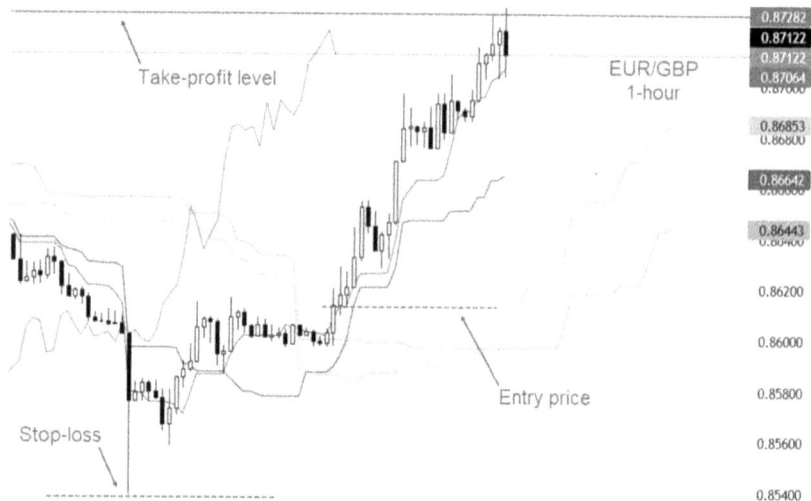

Figure 5-10: Trade example 2 - Take-profit level

Unlike the previous example, the price went quite smoothly in this retracement phase, and hardly had any difficulty in reaching the price target. Again, the profit level was when the price touched the Kijun-Sen in the longer timeframe. However, I am showing the price action on the 1-hour chart so that you can get a better idea of how the price move during the retracement stage.

It should also be noted that the risk-reward ratio is not quite good when we choose to trade the retracement phase. From my experience, it often falls around 1: 1.5 due to the short movement phase. Yet, to me, it's a high win-rate strategy where you can combine the power of multiple-timeframe analysis.

Let's take a look at another example:

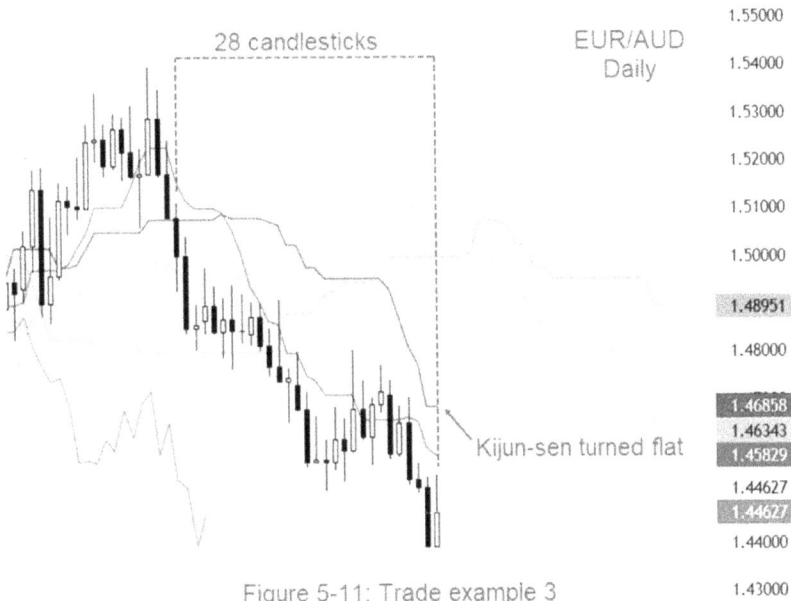

28 candlesticks

EUR/AUD
Daily

1.55000
1.54000
1.53000
1.52000
1.51000
1.50000
1.48951
1.48000
1.46858
1.46343
1.45829
1.44627
1.44627
1.44000
1.43000

Kijun-sen turned flat

Figure 5-11: Trade example 3

This is the EUR/AUD daily chart. It had been 28 candlesticks since the last Kijun-Sen – price touch. The Kijun-Sen turned flat, and we switch to the 1-hour frame to see what happened at that time.

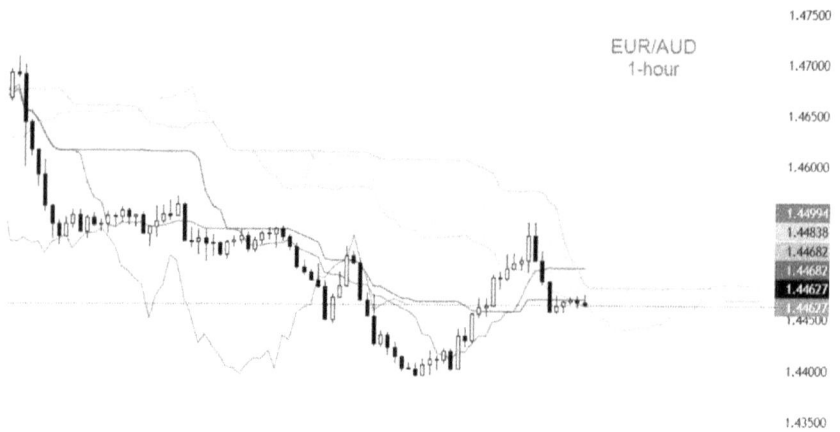

Figure 5-12: Trade example 3

The price was approaching the Kumo which became quite narrow at that point. I would say this is one of the most favorable conditions for a Kumo breakout under the Ichimoku context. We'll place an entry after the price broke the Kumo upwards, the stop-loss should be below the latest swing low, and the take profit will be the touch between the price and Kijun-Sen on the daily chart. These points are illustrated in the figure below.

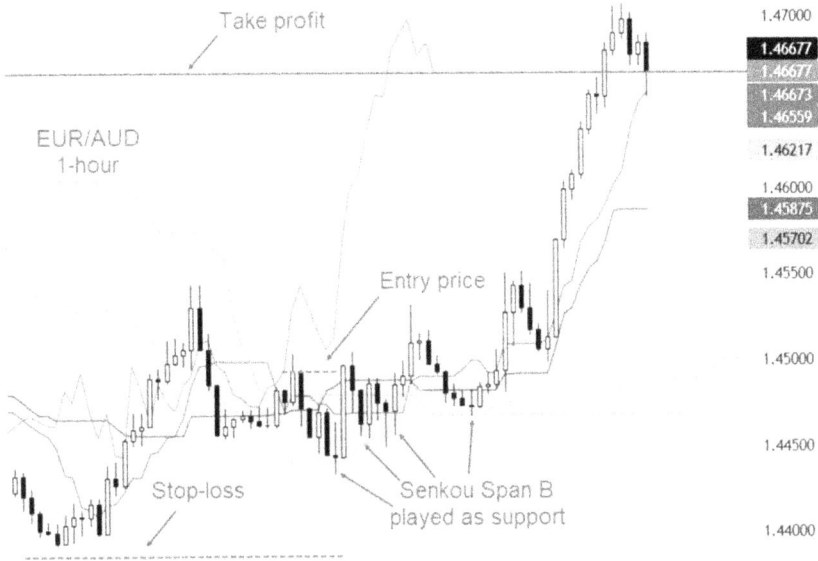

Figure 5-13: Trade example 3 - entry, stop, target

You can see that after the entry, the price experienced some choppy movements, but it never crossed below the Kumo. In other words, the Senkou Span B played as support several times, preventing the price to poke through the last defense of the bull trend over the short-term. Once the bear strength was denied by the bulls, the price skyrocketed through the target price level which was determined in the longer timeframe (the daily chart).

As always, it is recommended to refer to the forecast line in the daily chart to further verify the strength of the retracement phase. If the price remains above the line in an uptrend retracement, or below the line in a downtrend retracement, then we can say the retracement has been progressing well.

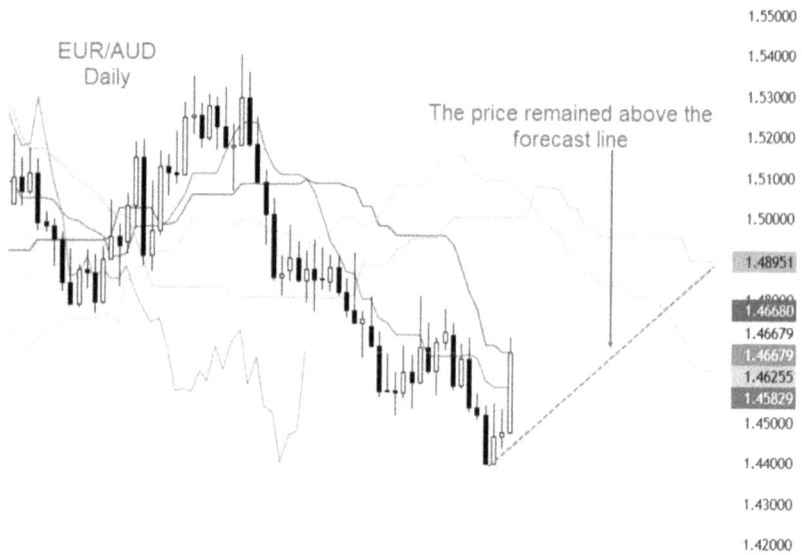

EUR/AUD
Daily

The price remained above the
forecast line

1.55000
1.54000
1.53000
1.52000
1.51000
1.50000
1.48951
1.46680
1.46679
1.46679
1.46255
1.45829
1.45000
1.44000
1.43000
1.42000

Figure 5-14: Trade example 3 - the forecast line

In this example, the price needs only three days to reach the Kijun-Sen (with three bullish candlesticks). This partly explains why the price didn't have any difficulty in remaining completely above the forecast line. Yet, in case of choppy and prolonged price movements, the comparison of price with the forecast line could provide more insights into the strength of the pullback.

Note:

- This is the rare case when I suggest a clear take-profit level without referring to other chart components. We cannot tell in which way the price may go after retracing to the Kijun-Sen. It may continue its retracement move, or resume the dominant trend. You shouldn't be too regretted when the Kijun-Sen makes a (much) deeper retracement, for example to the Kumo territory.

- The same principle can also be applied to Tenkan-Sen retracement trading. However, we all know that the Tenkan-Sen calculation is connected with running 9 periods, meaning that the price may retrace back to Tenkan-Sen in a very short time. Hence, I don't really prefer to counter-trend trade with the Tenkan-Sen.

- The amount of profit in each trade depends on which timeframe you'll start with. For example, if you start with the weekly timeframe and then enter the trade at the daily frame or 4-hour frame, you might enjoy (much) more profits compared to starting with the daily and entering the trade at the 1-hour chart.

- This strategy would be suitable for a number of financial markets. However, I tend not to apply it to highly volatile markets like cryptocurrency, or even the forex market amid major news releases. These are when the stop-loss is more vulnerable to being hit.

- This strategy is applicable in a trending market. It's when we look for a retracement phase after a prolonged move with the dominant trend. In a sideways market, the strategy is not recommended. In fact, I've never been a fan of trading in a sideways/range-bound market.

So, we've explored the second strategy using the combination of Kijun-Sen, multiple timeframe analysis, Kumo break, and the forecast line. The setups based on this strategy won't be as popular as in the first strategy where you can ride the trend and let profits run. Yet, based on a number of favorable factors, including the multiple timeframe analysis and the lesser-known philosophy of price retracement to Kijun-Sen, this method could be extremely useful in trading the pullbacks after a prolonged trending market. Once again, the key points in using this strategy successfully come from a close observation of the price movements and reactions in the market. Good opportunities don't come easily. Be patient and analyze the price action carefully with the help of the mid-term equilibrium price – Kijun-Sen.

The next chapter will surely bring you more "aha" moments where a lot of trading elements and techniques will be employed to produce the most appropriate trading options.

CHAPTER 6: DOUBLE THE ICHIMOKU POWER

Until now, we've focused mainly on the magic of the five lines in the Ichimoku context. Most books and websites out there will concentrate only on the five lines while forgetting the presence of the three theories. In fact, the three theories that we've learned in the previous chapters provide a comprehensive view of the market. The wave principle helps us better recognize the correlation between buyers and sellers. The price theory provides potential levels of support and resistance for profit-taking purposes. Meanwhile, the time theory provides a different angle in reading the price action with high-probability reversal zones, and traders can benefit from the time theory even before the price reaches certain zones on the chart.

In this chapter, we'll shift our focus on these three theories and the price action, with the help of the five lines to manage trades. You'll learn some new concepts in identifying the strength of a trend so that you can determine whether you should add more trades to your portfolio. This chapter will present a comprehensive strategy where we utilize the power of different tools and techniques. The strategy is highly customized to suit different trading types. Therefore, you'll certainly benefit from it regardless of your risk-tolerance degree.

Trade analysis

The wave theory will be the cornerstone that we use with our strategy in this chapter. The main function of the wave theory is to help us understand the structure of price action and how that structure is relating to the imbalance between the buyers and the sellers.

We're going to talk about how we can use wave theory for predictive analysis of future price action, why we need to understand the series of wave structures, what the structure means, and analyze when that structure is broken.

As we already know, there are three types of waves: I wave which is a single leg, V wave which is a double-I leg, and N wave which consists of an I and a V. As we've learned, a typical N wave would consist of four points A-B-C-D, and D is lower than B in a downtrend and higher than B in an uptrend. Failing to do that, the N wave structure is broken and the trend momentum is endangered. In other words, we would want to see a series of higher highs and higher lows in an uptrend, and a series of lower highs and lower lows in a downtrend. The consecutive lows and highs signal the imbalance between buyers and sellers in the market. In the following section, we'll start to tie in how the moves of waves translate into an imbalance of order flow.

Now, let's discover three types of wave patterns that we need to pay attention to when analyzing the waves in combination with the price action.

Wave structure holding (WSH)

Let's take a look at the chart below. To make this a little easier, we're using a clean chart with the Kumo only. *Wave structure holding* means for an N wave to occur, the following conditions need to be met.

- D point is higher than B in an uptrend and lower than B in a downtrend.
- C point is higher than A in an uptrend and lower than A in a downtrend.

As long as these conditions are satisfied, the wave structure is intact.

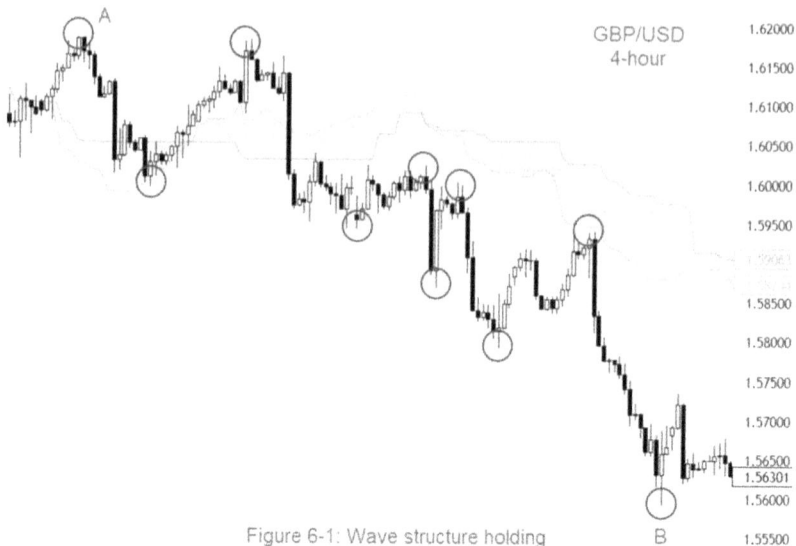

Figure 6-1: Wave structure holding

In this example, we can see a series of wave structure holding in a down-trending market. In other words, the price action forms consecutive lower highs and lower lows. The fact that the N wave structure keeps holding means we should be looking for more bearish trades than bullish trades until that structure is disrupted. In this chart, if we're taking 10 trades from A to B, around 80% of them should be bearish. As long as the wave structure is holding in one particular direction, we should be looking to be on that side of the market.

Wave structure advancing (WSA)

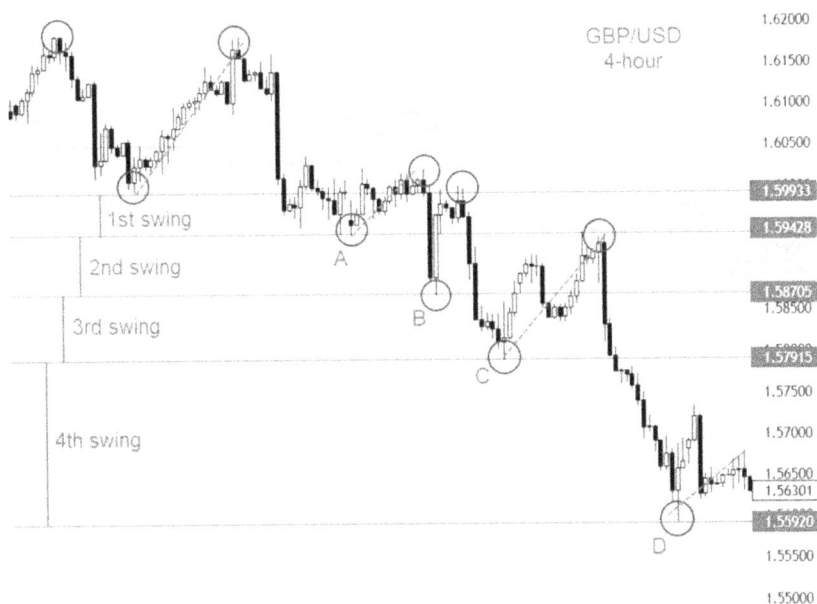

Figure 6-2: Wave structure advancing

There is also a hidden concept in the example above called *wave structure advancing*: the increase in the imbalance between buyers and sellers. On the chart above, we can see A makes a moderate new low, B makes a slightly bigger low, C makes a slightly bigger low, and then D is a significantly lower low. Moreover, look at how the retracements become less steep during the period. A *wave structure advancing* is characterized by (1) a bigger magnitude in the newly formed lows or highs, or (2) the angle of the retracement, or both.

In this case, wave structure advancing means the imbalance is increasing towards the bear side, and the bull side is in danger. It's just like the following game between two people: A and B. Supposed they're standing in front of each other, and A pushes B back five feet while B pushes A back 10 feet. If they just keep going at that back and forth, we can see who's going to lose that battle. Eventually, the person who gets pushed back further (A) is going to run out of power and fails to counteract that stronger force. Once that moment happens, there is what we call *capitulation*. It's a point where one side of the market gives

105

up from trying to push back on the market and says "Okay, we're gonna sit aside until you have exhausted yourself".

In the example above, once we've noticed the wave structure advancing, we should consider increasing the amount of time that we stay bearish in the market. This means you would want to look for fewer bull trades and more bear trades. If a wave structure is advancing in our favor, we should be more patient and willing to let the trade run a little longer.

Wave structure disruption (WSD)

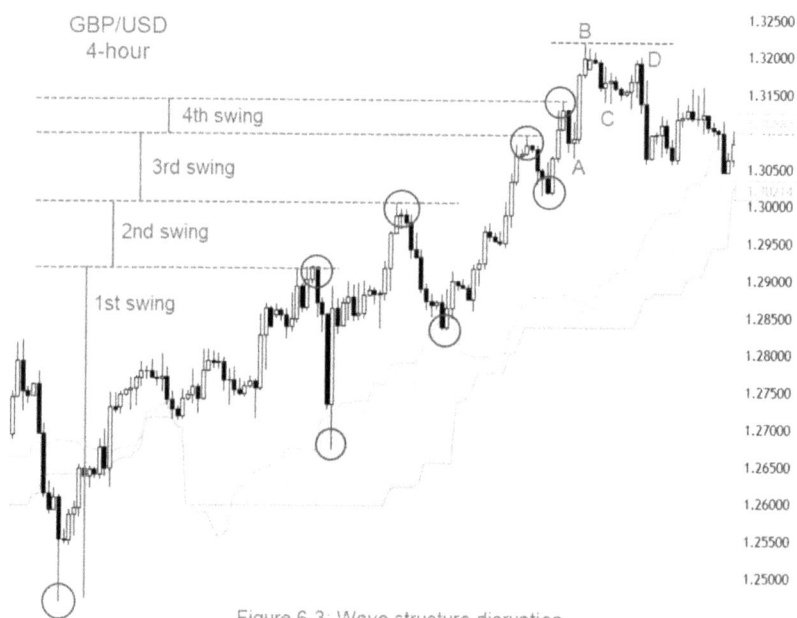

Figure 6-3. Wave structure disruption

The last type of wave pattern is wave structure disruption (WSD). Wave structure disruption means that there's a breakdown in the wave pattern. There are *two key points* for determining whether the structure is decaying. We still take a bullish price movement as an example. The same applies to bearish ones.

1. Is D the same or lower than B? If D is below or at the same price level as B, that would be the wave structure decaying.

106

2. Is C lower or at the same level as A? If yes, the wave structure has now been disrupted from the Ichimoku perspective.

The wave structure decaying tells that the imbalance is now shifting and becoming more neutralized. In the example above, I've circled most key price highs and lows during an uptrend. You can pick any four consecutive circled points and will find that the wave structure has been intact except for the last N wave where D is located below B. This marked the first official signal of a potential reversal. As you can see, soon after the WSD occurs, the candlestick closes inside the Kumo for the first time since the Kumo break.

Moreover, notice how the swings become gradually smaller during the course of the trend, which is opposite to the WSA pattern. This further suggests that the bullish trend won't last for long, especially after the fourth swing. Hence, even when the WSD doesn't occur, we should be able to anticipate an imminent reversal in the market.

Wave structure decaying is great from a predictive standpoint. When it happens, we should remain on the sidelines. If we've taken some long trades, and all of a sudden, the wave structure disrupts, that would be something like "Hold on a second! I need to pause and reassess at this point before taking any new longs, or consider taking profit at this point…" Wave structure disruption is a very important concept for us because it provides a predictive ability in terms of what is more likely for the price action.

With that being said, we've grasped another fresh view of wave patterns in the market. Now, let's see how wave patterns can be combined with different tools and techniques to establish a complete trading strategy.

Trade execution

In this section, we'll learn three methods of identifying the entry, stop-loss, and profit-taking prices, depending on traders' risk tolerance degree. While the three theories play an important part in identifying trade opportunities, we would also need to base on the five lines for trade purposes. We'll need to look at one of the three possible entry methods based on the wave structure. They are aggressive, moderate, and conservative tactics.

Aggressive method

Below are the steps for trading with the aggressive method:

-   Identifying the time cycle on the chart. A time cycle is ideally connected with a Kihon-suchi number (9, 26, 52, etc). However, it is not a hard and fast rule, meaning there can be a small difference to these Kihon-suchi numbers (1 or 2). If the time cycle is 9, there should be only one candlestick difference to be recognized as a valid time cycle.

-   Look for an N wave. Carefully observe the initial legs of the wave movement. Our target is to catch the last leg of the N wave, which may follow the time cycle.

-   The target entry price is the C point. We'll need to combine with the five-line context to find a possible entry for the trade, and no rule is hard and fast in this case.

-   The stop-loss would be based on price action and the shape of Kumo. It can be placed at the other side of the Kumo (if the Kumo is not quite large) or in the middle of the Kumo (if the Kumo is big), or just above the latest swing high (in case of a downtrend) below the latest swing low (in case of an uptrend) if the considered wave is a wave structure holding pattern.

-   The profit-taking level would be targeted on the nearest time cycle in the vertical axis. Concerning the profit-taking along with the horizontal axis, it would be determined when there is a wave structure disruption or be based on the four methods in the price observation theory.

The aggressive entry method gives the highest in terms of profitability but the least in terms of information from the market. It takes more skill and confidence in one's ability to adopt this kind of trade. It's considered the most aggressive because we are trying to catch it at the highest part of the C point which we don't know in advance. This is the reason we have to combine the wave theory with Ichimoku lines. The C point will have to match up to some other portions of the lines. It could be the Kumo that matches with the end of the C point, but it could also be the Kijun-Sen or Tenkan-Sen. The C point won't be determined until we have another leg down, and we are using a speculative method to get into it. This is why it's an aggressive option. You're probably going to be the least accurate in this, but once you win these trades, you're going to make the most money possible because they give you the best entry possible.

In short, with the aggressive tactic, we're trying to capture closest to the high of the C pullback in a bullish retracement and closest to the low of the C pullback in a bearish retracement. Theoretically, the C point can be one of these points: Kijun-Sen, Tenkan-Sen, Senkou Span A, and Senkou Span B. Normally, I tend to avoid catching the C point at the Senkou Span B because as I stated, trading inside the Kumo would be risky. Hence, if the retracement momentum turns out to be so strong that it violates the Kumo, we're going to shift to the second method: the moderate method.

Moderate method

Below are the steps for trading with the aggressive method:

- Identifying the time cycle on the chart. A time cycle is ideally connected with a Kihon-suchi number (9, 26, 52, etc). However, it is not a hard and fast rule, meaning there can be a small difference to these Kihon-suchi numbers (1 or 2; if the time cycle is 9, there should be only one candlestick difference to be recognized as a valid time cycle).

- Look for an N wave. Carefully observe the initial legs of the wave movement. Our target is to catch the last leg of the N wave, which may follow the time cycle.

- The target entry price would closely base on the Tenkan-Sen and/or Kijin-sen (notice there are cases when the price won't retrace to Kijun-Sen, hence we only need Tenkan-Sen for trading purposes). Specifically, we would wait for the price to cross past at least one of these two lines during its pullback phase, and then enter the trade when the price continues its movement with the dominant trend and cross back past the two lines. Doing this, we've determined the C point within the N wave structure before entering our trade, which is different from the aggressive method. Again, with the aggressive strategy, we don't have any idea of the end of the retracement (the C point) in advance.

  Moreover, the entry must be below the Kumo in a downtrend and above the Kumo in an uptrend. As I mentioned, I'm not interested in entering a storm, simple as that.

- The stop-loss would be above the C point or the Senkou Span A of the price in case of a bear trade, or below the C point or the Senkou Span A in case of a bull trade, depending on each market condition.

- The profit-taking level would be targeted on the nearest time cycle in the vertical axis. Concerning the profit-taking along with the horizontal axis, it would be determined when there is a wave structure disruption or be based on the four methods of the price observation theory.

Similar to the prior method, the moderate method entails relying on the C point. However, we would use the Tenkan-Sen and/or Kijin-Sen as supplemental factors in making our trade decision.

Let's say the market is bearish, and you've missed the C point as defined in the aggressive method. Yet, you believe the market is most likely to form a new low. The moderate entry would be determined after the price crosses back down below the Tenkan-Sen and Kijun-Sen. Ideally, starting from B, the price would need to cross above the Kijun-Sen and/or Tenkan-Sen during the correction period, and then cross back down below both lines to signal a possible continuation of the trend. That would mean the price hits resistance and then sold off. With the wave structure intact, we would be assuming that the market's going to make a new leg down. This method means lesser profitability but more Ichimoku supporting elements in place to confirm the price action.

Conservative method

Below are the steps for trading with the aggressive method:

- Identifying the time cycle on the chart. A time cycle is ideally connected with a Kihon-suchi number (9, 26, 52, etc). However, it is not a hard and fast rule, meaning there can be a small difference to these Kihon-suchi numbers (1 or 2; if the time cycle is 9, there should be only one candlestick difference to be recognized as a valid time cycle). Also, the cycle could also be connected with a Taito Suchi number.

- Look for an N wave. Carefully observe the initial legs of the wave movement. Our target is to catch the last leg of the N wave, which may follow the time cycle.

- The entry price is quite straightforward: when the price breaks the B level on its way to resume the trend. This method adds one big important signal to determine the entry price target – the B breakout point. Moreover, the entry with this method needs to be below the Kumo in case of a downtrend, and above the Kumo in case of an uptrend.

- The stop-loss could be above the C point if the trade is bearish, and below the C point if the trade is bullish. Where the B-C retracement phase is shallow, you can consider placing the stop price just above/below the Senkou Span A, depending on which direction you're trading.

- The profit-taking level would be targeted on the nearest time cycle in the vertical axis. Concerning the profit-taking along with the horizontal axis, it would be determined when there is a wave structure disruption or be based on the four methods of the price observation theory.

The most **conservative entry** would be a crossing below/above the B point. Notice it wouldn't be on a candle close but on a price break below that. Once the price breaks below/above the B price level, we're looking to go short. This method gives you the least amount of profitability and may require you to place a large stop. The upside of the method is that by breaking the B price level, we can be pretty sure that it's going to make a new low/high, and any pullback isn't going to get near the prior C point (the wave structure holds). Our **stop** from the Ichimoku perspective has to be quite large - just a few pips above/below the prior C point in most cases.

With the conservative method, we'll try to target two things.

First, by taking out the B low, we've tripped the stops of the bulls/bears that pushed the market back.

Second, we're hoping to get good momentum via a break through a key price level. If things aren't supportive initially, we'll turn our attention to any bounce heading to the C point. Because we're assuming that it's not going to reach the C point again, it's going to lead to another leg in the direction of the dominant trend. In short, we're trying to capture either an instant momentum or wait a little bit and capture the next leg up/down.

To me, I prefer the aggressive or the moderate method. The conservative technique isn't my style because it requires a massive stop and reduces some profits. However, it produces a better win rate as compared to the other two. The conservative method would be more suitable for risk-averse or newbie traders.

Note: Regarding the first step - *identifying a time cycle on the chart*: at least two consecutive cycles are recommended to confirm a valid time cycle. If you are a conservative trader, you might want to increase the number to three. On the other hand, one newly formed cycle isn't enough for time cycle confirmation purposes.

Trade examples

Now, let's move to some trade examples to better grasp the great combination between Ichimoku lines and theories.

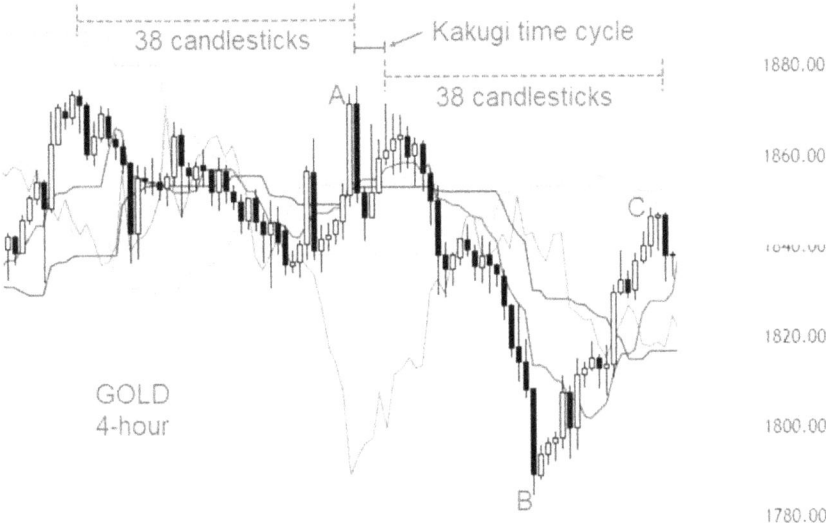

Figure 6-4: Trade example 1

This is the 4-hour chart of Gold. Currently, we've seen a V wave A-B-C in a bear trend bias. Notice the C point locates just below the Senkou Span A – an ideal position for the end of a reversal. At this point, what we look for is one more leg toward the dominant trend to complete an N wave.

Now, let's talk about the time theory. A quick scan of the chart can provide us with a Kakugi time cycle (38-candlestick cycle) where there is a small space between the two cycles. Notice that we assume the C point has been found, so we're not going to find an aggressive trade entry anymore. Based on the latest price action, our possible target is a trade entry based on the moderate method. This is when the price crosses below both Tenkan-Sen and Kijun-Sen, and it must close below the Kumo as well. In the next chart, we can find an entry that satisfies all these conditions.

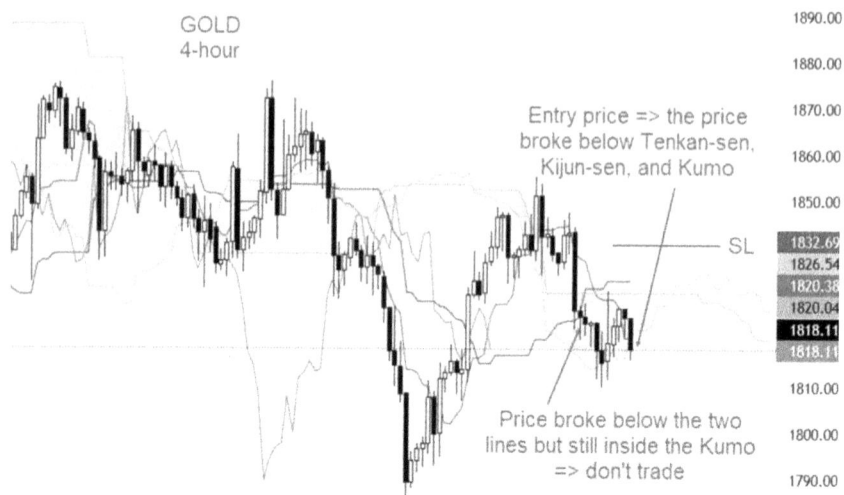

Figure 6-5: Trade example 1 - entry price

It should be noted that the price didn't go down right away. The market experienced some volatilities before entering the Kumo with a long candlestick, and what we expect to be the C point turned out to be a false C point (the price managed to break the Kumo afterward and formed another swing high – the end of the retracement). However, since we aim to trade under the moderate method, we're all safe. This is how a careful analysis can save us many times in the market.

Coming back to the Kumo, as I mentioned earlier, we don't enter any trade with the moderate method until the price exits the Kumo cloud. The break occurred soon afterward although it wasn't a decisive break. This is when we could enter a trade. The stop-loss should be placed on the other side of the Kumo. I prefer not to place it just a few pips above the cloud because it started to shrink at that point (not a big Kumo).

The take-profit target should first be based on the next time cycle. Look at the chart below.

114

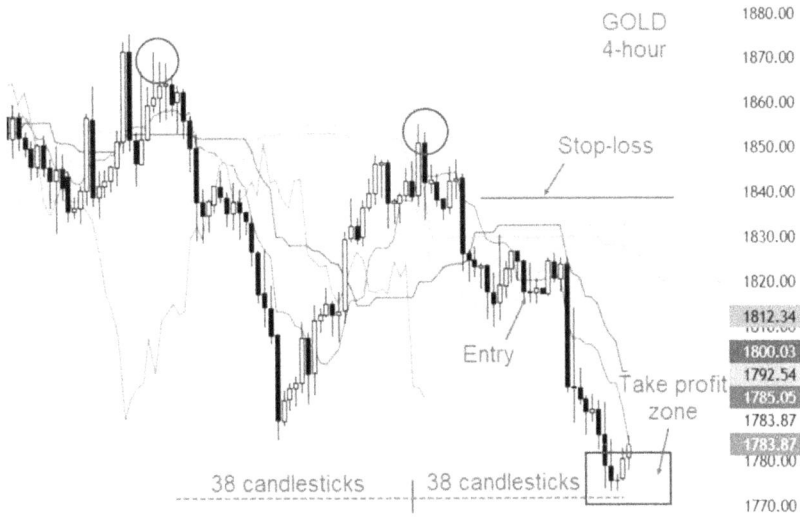

Figure 6-6: Trade example 1 - Take profit

Remember that the market had been moving within the 38-candlestick cycle, hence we should bear in mind that after 38 candlesticks from the end of the last cycle, there might be a key price swing. In this example, the time theory is completely respected where the price made a minor retracement to reach the Tenkan-Sen equilibrium point. We can choose any profit-taking price within the target zone and secure a decent profit.

Now, the beauty of this method is that you can utilize past price actions to anticipate the next possible price target. Notice in the chart above, the C points remained outside the Kumo (the circled ones), with the second one closer to the Kumo. At this point, we might expect the next C point might be around the Senkou Span B and didn't fall outside the Kumo, considering the diminishing retracement momentum that happened in the financial markets quite often. Look at the next example below.

115

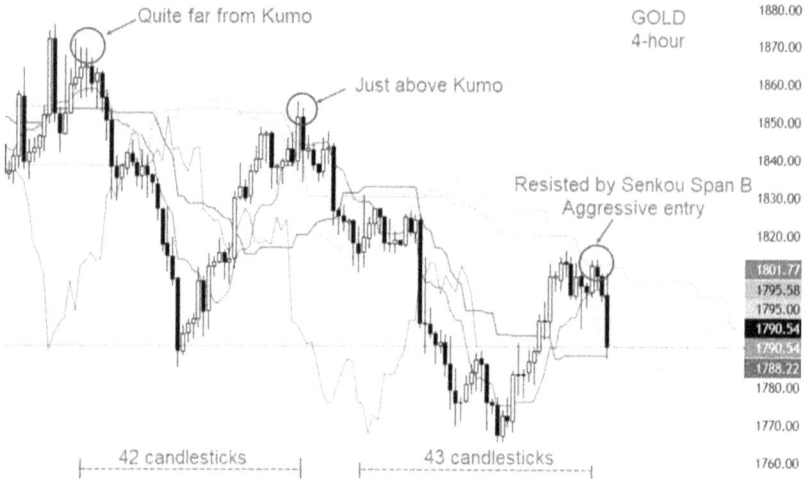

Figure 6-7: Trade example 1 - anticipating the next C point

In this example, we've refreshed the chart a little bit and can find a 42-candlestick cycle between the nearest two swing highs. Then, with the expectation that the next pullback wouldn't exceed the Senkou Span B and a possible time cycle in mind, we can find a trade entry right at the Senkou Span B as indicated. Notice the refreshed time cycle is once again a Kakugi time cycle. The bottom in this downtrend locates near the end of the 43-candlesticks cycle as in the chart below.

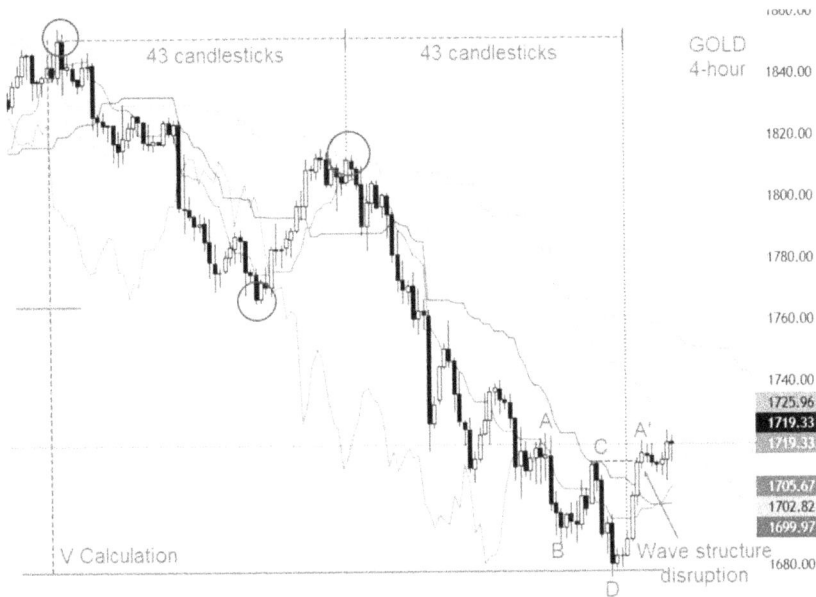

Figure 6-8: Trade example 1 - Take profit

Looking at the chart, you can see how powerful the time cycle is in identifying a possible price reversal in the market. Also, a wave structure disruption is occurring soon after the market formed the bottom. Notice how A' is higher than the C point of the previous N wave. Even if you choose to take profit based on the wave structure disruption, you've gone a long way with the downtrend and made a decent profit. Last but not least, by using the price theory (the V calculation) with the first three points circled on the chart, we can also determine a price target right at bottom of the downtrend. We call it the confluence effect where many techniques produce the same result.

So, in this example, we've incorporated two types of methods (aggressive and moderate) in trading with a bear trend, with a close combination between the theories and the Ichimoku lines. Also, note that the financial markets are characterized by their volatilities. Hence, it's advisable that we revise the time cycle at some points during the progression of the trend. In other words, we should look at wave progressions from different angles, which in turn helps us to make better use of price actions.

Let's look at another example.

117

Figure 6-9: Trade example 2

This is the daily chart of GBP/JPY. The price broke the Kumo downwards and the Chikou line was below the price, indicating the bears had taken control of the market. From the top of the chart, the market formed consecutive lower highs and lower lows shaped into N wave structures. At first glance, a wave structure holding pattern was in place. Notice that C is lower than A, and E is lower than C. If we count the wave structure from C, the market has formed the first three points of an N wave, and our aim is to trade with the last leg of the N wave.

Now, if we look at the swing highs, they tend to follow the time theory with a period of 26 candlesticks – a Kihon Suchi number. Note that there might be one or two candlestick differences, which is completely acceptable in determining the time cycle. If you've missed the aggressive entry at just below the Kijun-Sen, you can choose a moderate entry when the price crosses the Tenkan-Sen downward as indicated on the chart.

In many cases, the entry price could also be anticipated via what we call the diminishing retracement momentum. We mentioned it in the previous example. On this chart, we can see the A retracement occurred completely above Kumo. Then, the B-C retracement ended just below the Senkou Span B.

118

Finally, the D-E retracement ended just below the Tenkan-Sen. You'll see the weaker momentum in price retracement quite frequently on the chart. This plays an important add-on or supportive element in determining the end of a retracement phase and finding an appropriate entry level.

Also, let's look at the swing lows. The two nearest swing lows are 30-bar away, so what we can expect is the continuation of this 30-bar cycle. This is also a potential take-profit target as the bear trend progresses. Now, let's see what happened next.

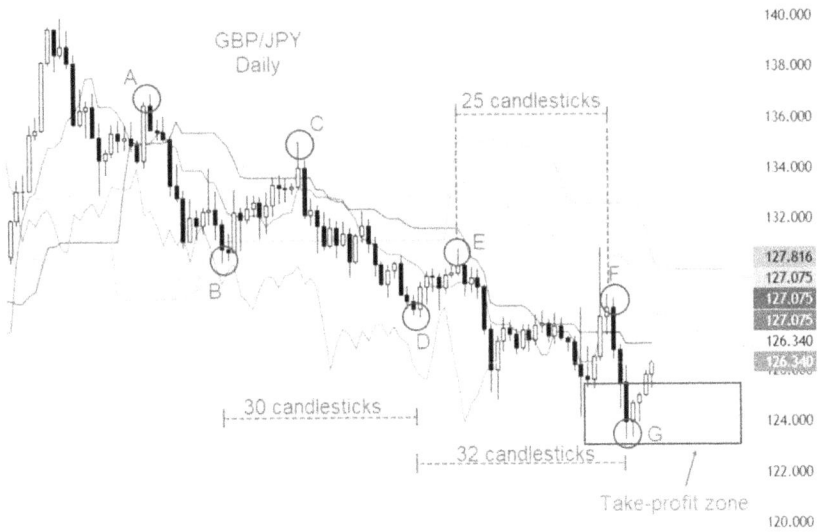

Figure 6-10: Trade example 2 - Take profit

This chart once again indicates the market's respect for the time principle. Another swing low was formed at G, and the D-G distance is 32 candlesticks, close to the 30-bar cycle during the previous phase. Hence, just by complying with the time cycle, we're able to catch an ideal take-profit price in this example. Moreover, notice how the latest swing high (F) also respects the Kihon-suchi time principle (the E-F distance includes 25 candlesticks – very close to the 26-bar time period). Ideally, in this example, we have two time cycles that were respected for a long trending move: a 26-bar one with swing highs and a 30-bar one with swing lows.

119

So, we've gone through the most comprehensive trading method in this book where we've learned how to combine the three Ichimoku theories with magical lines and the diminishing retracement momentum. There are three ways to enter a trade based on your risk tolerance degree. From my experience, you won't be a master of these techniques without observing and practicing with real charts many times. It might be long, but it's definitely worth it. Try to look at as many charts as possible, read what the market gives you, take notes, and stick to what you've learned.

CONCLUSION

Ichimoku has unfair advantages over other technical indicators. Its main advantage lies in the reflection of the equilibrium point in the market, giving us a reliable and fact-based idea of what may happen next in the market, and calculating a number of factors in consideration. This is the key difference from some other indicators which signify the overbought or oversold areas, which won't work quite well in a strong trending market.

By focusing on the market price, we can grasp a good picture of the battle between buyers and sellers, who is winning advantage, who is showing some tiredness, etc. Moreover, it provides short-term, mid-term, and long-term views of what the market has been doing and how it may perform next. The three theories and the five-line context are connected with past, current, and future price action that can provide a comprehensive reflection of the market. We can hardly find any all-in-one system like Ichimoku among thousands of technical indicators out there. With Ichimoku Kinko Hyo, we can not only gain a good understanding of what the market is telling but also determine high-probability entry, exit, and stop-loss levels. This is the reason Ichimoku is considered a complete trading system.

The three strategies have been optimized and customized to suit traders' styles. All strategies reflect great combinations of both Ichimoku lines and price actions and are the results of years of back-testing with real examples. They might seem complex at first where many steps are involved, however, when you start getting familiar with them, you can identify trade opportunities as well as how to enter and exit trades at a glance.

Unlike other trading systems where price targets are often "above this" or "below that", using Ichimoku requires you to be flexible to make use of the system the best way. A typical example of this is the Kumo whose width reflects the strength of the trend to some extent. By looking at the Kumo and how it changes over time, we could find an appropriate stop-loss for our trade instead of a hard and fast price target rule. This is one of the most valuable points brought about by Ichimoku Kinko Hyo because it reflects the cornerstone quality when trading: *flexibility*.

I hope you've enjoyed every part of this book and are ready to apply what I've presented in real trading. This is not a quick process, and you'll need a lot of practice, refreshing, and optimization before truly understanding the tool and making consistent profits. Furthermore, although I've tried to open some different trade options, you can customize more to best suit your trading style. Remember trading's not about 'do this" or "do that". Trading is about how you understand what the market is telling in an objective way in each situation. The best way to grasp a good understanding of the market is by investigating price action, the buyer-seller correlation, and the equilibrium price of the market. The Ichimoku technique, with the combination of different views, offers you all these functions in the most intuitive way.

This brings us to the end of the book. I want to congratulate you on finishing this book, and strongly believe that you've made the right decision in taking your trading skills to the next level. Now, it's time to take consistent actions.

Finally, if you find you've learned something useful in this book, please spend a few minutes of your treasured time leaving *an honest review* as a way to help other traders and learners.

JARROD SANDERS

ELLIOTT WAVE
FIBONACCI
**HIGH
PROBABILITY
TRADING**

MASTER THE WAVE PRINCIPLE AND MARKET TIMING
WITH PROVEN STRATEGIES

Scan this barcode to check out an ultimate Elliott Wave – Fibonacci trading guide.

REFERENCES

(2022, November 22). Ichimoku Kinko Hyo. Fincash.

https://www.fincash.com/l/basics/ichimoku-kinko-hyo

Mitchell, C. (2022, August 25). Tenkan-Sen (Conversion Line). Investopedia.

https://www.investopedia.com/terms/t/tenkansen.asp

Mitchell, C. (2022, August 25). Kijun-Sen (Base Line). Investopedia.

https://www.investopedia.com/terms/k/kijunsen.asp

Chen, J. (2022, January 31). Ichimoku Kinko Hyo. Investopedia.

https://www.investopedia.com/terms/i/ichimokuchart.asp

Mitchell, C. (2022, August 25). Chikou Span (Lagging Span). Investopedia.

https://www.investopedia.com/terms/c/chikouspan.asp

Mitchell, C. (2022, October 10). Senkou (Leading) Span B. Investopedia.

https://www.investopedia.com/terms/s/senkouspanb.asp

Mitchell, C. (2021, September 01). Senkou Span A (Leading Span A). Investopedia.

https://www.investopedia.com/terms/s/senkouspanb.asp

(2022, February 19). Best Ichimoku Strategy for Quick Profits. Tradingstrategyguides.

https://tradingstrategyguides.com/best-ichimoku-strategy/

Ichimoku Kinko Hyo. Earnforex

https://www.earnforex.com/forex-course/ichimoku-kinko-hyo/

Simmons, A. (2019, November 15). The Three Principles – Wave Principle. Forex.Academy.

https://www.forex.academy/the-three-principles-wave-principle/

Simmons, A. (2019, November 17). The Three Principles – Timespan Principle. Forex.Academy.

https://www.forex.academy/the-three-principles-timespan-principle/

Simmons, A. (2019, November 17). The Three Principles – Price Principle. Forex.Academy.

https://www.forex.academy/the-three-principles-price-principle/

Groette, O. (2022, October 10). Ichimoku Strategy. Quantified Strategies.

https://www.quantifiedstrategies.com/ichimoku-strategy/

Forex Trading Strategies With Ichimoku Kinko Hyo. Dolphintrader.

https://www.dolphintrader.com/forex-trading-strategies-with-ichimoku-kinko-hyo/

www.ingramcontent.com/pod-product-compliance
Lightning Source LLC
Chambersburg PA
CBHW071429210326

41597CB00020B/3718